BAPTISTS IN BURMA

RANDOLPH L. HOWARD, Associate Foreign Secretary of the American Baptist Foreign Mission Society, is a graduate of Shurtleff in the Class of 1905. After a term of three years as Greek and Latin Master in Broaddus Institute, he entered the Philosophy Department of Harvard University, and in 1910 received his A. M. degree. Immediately thereafter he sailed for Rangoon, Burma, to become Professor of Psychology in Judson College. It was the first year of full college work in that institution; the student body was small, and the college was struggling for recognition. During the fourteen years of Doctor Howard's service at Judson, he saw it grow to become one of the outstanding Mission Colleges of India.

A prominent athlete in his college days, he carried a fine spirit of sportsmanship to the playing fields of India, being the director of a large and varied athletic program not only in Judson College, but also in the three high schools allied with it during almost all of his service in Burma.

In 1920 political unrest in India brought on a disastrous student strike in Rangoon. Under the strain of those tense days, President Gilmore's health broke, as also did that of his successor, Doctor Kelly, after only three months' service. In the spring of 1921, Doctor Howard was elected President. The student body was sorely depleted, the future was uncertain, yet under his leadership Judson College was back to normal attendance within a few months, and showed steady growth during the years of his administration.

An outstanding achievement of that period was the successful carrying through of negotiations with the Burma Government whereby the continuance of Judson as a full college was secured. Doctor Howard also brought to definite fruition plans maturing for more than a decade whereby a magnificent new site of almost sixty acres was secured for Judson, together with a half million dollars pledged from Burma sources for buildings.

During these years, Doctor Howard was Chairman of the Executive Committee of the Burma Mission, and a member of the Senate of the University of Rangoon. He also served on many important committees of the provincial education department.

In 1924 a break in Mrs. Howard's health compelled a return to America, and the slowness of her recovery compelled Doctor Howard to present his resignation. He then accepted appointment to the Administrative Staff of the American Baptist Foreign Mission Society. There was at that time still to be secured the half million dollars from America needed to meet the pledges obtained in Burma for the Judson College buildings. Doctor Howard has been able to do his part in bringing that campaign to a successful conclusion. Judson will shortly have an exceptionally fine plant easily worth three millions if built in America.

Doctor Howard's present position gives him important responsibilities in the administration of mission work in India, Burma, China, Japan, and the Philippines.

A MORTON LANE GIRL

BAPTISTS IN BURMA

By RANDOLPH L. HOWARD

Edited by
The Department of Missionary Education
Board of Education of the Northern Baptist Convention
152 Madison Avenue, New York City

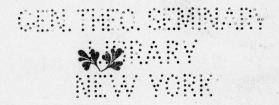
PHILADELPHIA
THE JUDSON PRESS

| BOSTON | CHICAGO | LOS ANGELES |
| KANSAS CITY | SEATTLE | TORONTO |

PRINTED IN U. S. A.

FOREWORD

The power of the Christian message to transform a pagan country into a Christian commonwealth is nowhere more convincingly demonstrated than in the land of Burma. From the first day of Judson's arrival until now, Burma has been a land of promise. Judson's first little flock of nineteen converts has become a Christian community of more than one-quarter million. Superstition has yielded to education. Churches, schools, hospitals, asylums, and philanthropies have conspired to show the native enterprise of this land to which we sent our first missionaries.

Burma holds the promise of a new day in her national life, and her desire for independent political status is soon to be satisfied. The Christian movement in Burma continues to be one of significant promise. Mr. Howard, with his broad knowledge gained through years of experience, makes some interesting predictions on Burma's future.

This book is full of vivid word pictures and panoramic descriptions, showing the changing life of this people under Christianity's influence. As a reading book, *Baptists in Burma* has the charm of a continued story; as a book of inspiration, it looks toward a larger land of promise—the Christian conquest of the Orient; as a

FOREWORD

source-book, it has the value of a compendium of information; as a study-book, it has the teaching quality of a trustworthy record.

In connection with the study of " Christianity and Rural Life Around the World," *Baptists in Burma* demonstrates the far-reaching influence of Christianity in a great rural State.

We heartily commend this timely book to the attention of adults and young people for missionary reading and study.

WILLIAM A. HILL.

CONTENTS

CONTENTS

CONTENTS

LIST OF ILLUSTRATIONS

I

ADONIRAM JUDSON

Judson, 1813

" Just at night " on Tuesday the thirteenth of July, 1813, Adoniram Judson stood in the " Water Gate " of Rangoon. His was a solitary figure. For loneliness it can hardly be equalled in the history of any great cause. He and Ann Hasseltine, his wife, must that day decide a question, most vital not merely to themselves but to American Baptists as well. Behind him some sixty feet of slimy mud bank fell away to a broad bend of the Rangoon River. In this spacious harbor there rode at anchor the sailing ship which had just brought them to Burma. Before him stood a stockade, and through the gate he glimpsed a city, a sprawling mass of thatch-roofed huts. Each was set high on stilts out of harm's way when the tides belched forth filthy water from the intersecting creeks. Formerly a much fairer city, fire and misgovernment had reduced it from thirty to perhaps eight thousand people. As the sun, up river, dropped below the horizon Judson must have heard the squealing " meager swine " as they, the day shift of scavengers, turned over their duties to the howling packs of pariah dogs soon to make the night hideous. The first sight of the city was not pleasant for a prospective resident. William Carey back in Calcutta had warned him. His son Felix and his associates had undergone sore trials there. This warning had caused Judson to regard Rangoon with a feeling of "horror." Evidently half the horrors had not been told. Could they, even as his wife hoped, be "instrumental in removing some of the rubbish and preparing the way for others"? Could they succeed where the English brethren had failed? Felix Carey, he found, had been summoned to the king's court at distant Ava. There was little likelihood of his return to mission work. No visible evidence of the five English Baptists remained save the mission residence and the grave of Mr. Brian.

Too, the Judsons had no assured financial support. Study of the Scripture during the seventeen weeks from Boston to Calcutta had convinced them that theirs was not "believers' baptism." After baptism by immersion in the Lal Bazar Chapel in Calcutta, there had gone that letter to the American Board. Their connections with the Congregationalists with "everything to allure," had been severed. Could and would American Baptists assume their support? Lake Champlain had hitherto been the utmost limits of the missionary endeavor of Boston Baptists. The "ladies in Harvard" must increase their contribution of $4.87 if even his salary of $666.66 was to be met.

As the deep curtain of tropical night closed suddenly about him Judson turned back to board the Georgiana, there to face the severest test of all. Under a simple canvas shelter on the deck of that miserable craft lay Ann Hasseltine. She had faced death during the twenty-two tempestuous days from Madras. Rangoon offered neither medical attention nor congenial companionship. Mrs. Felix Carey might read both Burmese and Portuguese, but she could speak no English. Mrs. Newell, companion of the

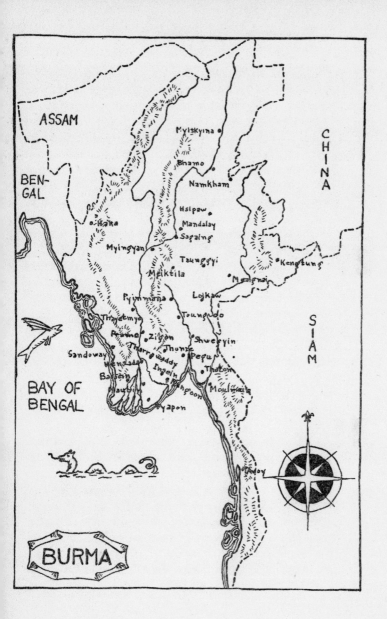

voyage to Calcutta, lay buried on the Isle of France. Had he any right to risk Ann's health further? Modern wisdom would have warned him not to set foot on shore. Yet the next day " Mrs. Judson, still too weak to walk, was carried into town." The die was cast. American Baptist foreign missions had that day their beginning in Burma.

Burma

Burma is a sort of blind alley. It is easy of approach only by sea. The most easterly of India's provinces, it is also much the largest. Lying beyond the Bay of Bengal, that wide sea is two-fifths of its boundary. The other three-fifths are formed by a series of mountain ranges. It is 1,200 miles in length. Victoria Point, the most southerly extremity, touches Malaysia. It reaches far north to the apex of the Triangle where Tibet and China meet. The total area of Burma is about that of the eleven States north of the Ohio and east of the Wabash Rivers. The long coast-line has great stretches of mud-flats and sandbanks. These make it unapproachable for ships of any size except where the main streams keep a channel open. In many places are belts of mangroves in the soft mud. They are so often inundated at high tide that oysters live on the trees. At the far south are clusters of islands as picturesque as any in the Inland Sea of Japan.

Burma may be divided from a physical point of view into three parts. The western includes Arakan along the Bay of Bengal and the Chin and Kachin Hills. The eastern is the Shan States, Karenni and the Province of Tenasserim. The central includes the Irrawaddy basin, a dry zone about and below Mandalay covered largely with scrub jungle, and the Irrawaddy delta extending back up as far as Prome. This last is one of the rich garden spots of the world.

Mountains and Rivers

The mountains which wall in Burma on three sides begin back up in Tibet on the roof of the world. They extend in the form of a pitchfork with the basin of the Irrawaddy between the two prongs. One prong forms the eastern frontier. The other is the Yomas, separating Arakan from the rest of Burma. Some of these mountains are eleven thousand feet above sea-level. Many of them are covered with almost impenetrable forests. The chief river is the Irrawaddy. It is one of the most noble rivers in Asia. Its upper defiles are magnificent. Below Mandalay there is much flat and uninteresting country, but from Prome on, it intersects the delta with its many mouths. Here the beauty of its tree-covered banks is indescribable. It is the Irrawaddy which first greets the traveler to Burma by its yellow silt far out at sea.

The Salween is the second of the rivers in point of size. It, too, rises in the far north and, hemmed in by mountains, rushes to the sea through deep gorges. These are but two of Burma's large rivers. The Irrawaddy is preeminent because it is navigable for nine hundred miles.

Climate

The valleys of Burma have three seasons, the cool and dry weather, the hot weather, and the rains. These run into each other so that it is often hard to separate them. There is no question about the hot season, nor can one doubt the existence of the rains. Sandoway in a half year has 250 inches. It is sometimes a source of argument as to whether any cool season exists. Some years seemed divided into two seasons, the dry and the wet, both hot. From late May to the middle of October there is seldom a day without a downpour. It rarely rains during the remainder of the year. Humidity is almost always high. One seldom wishes to wear any but the lightest clothing. There is never a killing frost. Microbes multiply without let or hindrance.

Birds and Beasts

Space does not permit the mention of many of the birds and beasts. There are the white-browed gibbon of the north and the white-handed gibbon of the south. There are the little mouse-deer and the mighty elephant. Then there are the reptiles. On the very first night in Rangoon we were disturbed by a large snake chasing rats in the attic of the old bungalow. We were entertained by little lizards, the size of your finger, catching the insects on the ceiling. Almost all that one may imagine of tropical wild life is found in Burma.

Minerals

Burma has hardly the wondrous wealth early voyagers imagined. Still it is fairly rich in minerals. Gold and silver are found in the hills in the northeast. Mandalay has marble quarries. Mogok supplies the world with rubies. Jade and amber come from beyond Bhamo. Oil-derricks thickly dot the banks of the Irrawaddy half-way between Rangoon and Mandalay. It is not on minerals, however, but on the rice crop that most people depend. The soil with little care gives a fair yield. Just burn off last year's stubble, and it fertilizes sufficiently to assure a crop. This was enough for a comfortable living, as long as Burma's rice was in world-wide demand.

Burma's Chief Gateway

Eighty miles of muddy water greet the traveler to Burma before he passes Elephant Point and enters the mouth of the Rangoon River. It is twenty-one miles up this stream that the capital of the province is situated. To Rangoon's great wharves come many ocean steamers. To these wharves also come a large fleet of Irrawaddy Flotilla steamers. These ply the delta's many streams and also go up country as far as Bhamo. For miles above Monkey Point the Rangoon River is over a mile wide. It offers an ample harbor for shipping even at the height of the rice season. But before we survey Baptist mission work in Burma's chief city, let us have a further glimpse at the pioneers.

The Missionary Purpose

More than three years were to pass, it was 1816, before any recruits arrived from America to help the Judsons. There were even then but two, George and Phœbe Hough. Mr. Hough was a printer. Certain articles of agreement were drawn up by Judson, the eminent translator of the Burmese Bible, and Hough, the first to print its pages on Burmese soil. These reveal the propelling purpose of their hazardous enterprise. Their " sole object on earth," they declare, " is to introduce the religion of Jesus Christ into the empire of Burmah." The story of their accomplishments as translator and printer is to be told later. Adoniram Judson must be seen first in the rôle in which he is preeminent, that of a winner of men to his Master.

To him the printed word was essential. The spoken word was, however, the major means of attaining their objective. In both these ways few if any have displayed a patient persistence equal to Judson's. He pressed on in the face of seemingly insuperable obstacles. Settled among a people utterly untouched of Christ, he won them by the simple fragrance of his life and message.

First Converts

No more inspiring chapter is found in all the annals of American efforts to carry Christ across the seas than that of Judson's winning that first handful of converts in Rangoon. Run through the record of the first nineteen converts. Ann Hasseltine was carried through curious throngs on July 14, 1813. The nineteenth member was welcomed into the Rangoon Church on July 21, 1822. Nine soul-trying years! Almost four years passed before there was even the mention of an inquirer. No congregation gathered in the zayat, the little open preaching-shed beside Pagoda Road, till a Sunday morning in April of 1819. Thousands had passed along that wide festival thoroughfare to the great golden Shwe Dagon pagoda, but never before had more than three or four lingered to listen. It was that same April that the first convert, Maung Nau, came to the zayat. A vivid picture is painted of the baptism of this humble disciple three months later.

The more one studies the winning of that first nineteen the more one's admiration mounts. Piece together a paragraph here, a sentence there, and one finds what might well be called a case history of each. Judson, the physician of souls, emerges. As he threads the maze of an Oriental tongue his technique develops. First one possible approach is tested, then another. The effect of each phrase, each act, is watched with intense anxiety. Like a physician fascinated by a new and as yet unconquered tropical disease, every symptom is observed with anxious attention. Now he fears that his remedies are too drastic and that he has driven the inquirer away. Then again hope mounts high, for some word seems to have gripped the heart. His quiet persistence and infinite care never falter till the fight is won, a soul is saved. Outstanding among those first few is Maung Shwa Gnong. Entries culled from the pages of the Judson manuscripts give the case history of "the teacher," as Judson continually calls him. With each succeeding entry, admiration increases for America's first foreign missionary. It required eleven months of effort before the teacher was finally won.

The name of Maung Shwa Gnong should be placed with that of Judson on that "monument," the Burmese Bible, for it is impossible to see how that tremendous translation task could ever have been accomplished without his able assistance.

Converts Today

Judson's first nineteen converts called for nine years of heroic labor. For a striking contrast take the same nine years a century later: the years of 1913-1922 saw 33,350 brought into the membership of Baptist churches in Burma, while the census of this latter date gives a Christian community of nearly 260,000.

The one little Baptist church in 1822 has become in 1931 some 1,320 churches scattered far and wide, "introducing the religion of Jesus Christ" among the races of Burma hitherto "destitute of pure gospel light." Burma is a land of many tongues. The Burmese, by far the largest group, dominate the valleys. In the hills, spilling down into the valleys, are many other races. The call of such sturdy mountain men as the Karens, the Chins, and the Kachins are chapters in themselves. These lines of lesser resistance have been followed until the Karen Christians alone form a community of 179,000, and Christ is winning the hearts of Chins and Kachins in a way that gives real promise of those groups being brought almost bodily into the Kingdom. Among the Burmans, however, the race for which Judson and a great group of the world's finest missionaries have given themselves, is found a Christian community of only sixteen thousand. Yet the Burmese are well over nine of the thirteen million people of the province. These people, immersed in Buddhism, still need more " physicians of the soul " with the devotion of the Judsons to win them one by one to Christ. They do not come by villages or families. There are no mass movements as in India. There is a challenge to American Baptists today in the consecration of the members of her first expeditionary force overseas.

Judson, 1931

To Burma have come men of all races. On Rangoon's crowded thoroughfares may be found Chinese, Japanese, Malays, Siamese, natives of India of all the three score and ten varieties, together with Armenians, Jews, English, French, Germans, Italians, Greeks, and all the European nationalities. Mingled with these throngs of foreigners are the native races—Burmese, Talaings, Shans, and Karens. For any one who would study facial types, let him stand near the Sule Pagoda. It forms an island in

Rangoon's finest street. Around its base there swirls within the hour the world's most varied mixture of mankind. The different tongues have compelled a certain diversification of mission work. This is true to a degree in many parts of Burma. It is peculiarly so in Rangoon. Take then a hasty survey of Burma's capital and chief city. It is the main center of Baptist activity in Burma. It is also the largest center of Northern Baptist foreign missions found anywhere in the world.

On Merchant Street is the Mission Press; a block away facing Fytche Square is Immanuel Baptist Church; a couple of blocks east on Dalhousie Street stands the Union Hall School for immigrant Indians. Leaving the center of the city, out beyond Soratee Bazar is Lanmadaw. This " royal highway " church and school are direct descendants of Judson's first little flock. Some of Rangoon's finest folk are found in the church and on the staff of the school. But one cannot fail to feel a bit of shame at the buildings. Let us hurry on out Commissioner Road to where it becomes Lower Kemmendine Road. There is the old Judson College campus. The removal of Judson College leaves adequate room for the three allied schools which remain. Cushing High School is the mother of them all, including Judson College. The Normal School has trained many teachers from all over Burma. The English High School is for the Euro-Burmans, as the Anglo-Indians of Burma now call themselves. Swinging free of the city, we go out Mission Road into a residential suburb. Here is a great beehive of Baptist activity. It has seven mission bungalows, a missionary " rest-house," and many other buildings. The Burmese work there has two bungalows, one for the women missionary evangelists, and one for the evangelistic family for the Rangoon field. Together with these are the Lanmadaw parsonage and the Fredrickson Memorial for Burmese Bible Women. For the Karens there are likewise two bungalows, together with the Brayton Memorial, the building of the Bible School for Karen Women, and Pegu Karen High School—a fine group of buildings centering in the Vinton Memorial. Still our survey is not ended. A couple of miles west, beyond the idol-carvers' quarter, is Kemmendine Girls School, ministering to all races. Then, last but not least, a mile or more farther west on the Victoria Lakes is Judson College. To all these institutions we must return before we leave Burma. Let us pause just a moment more at the college.

The new fifty-four-acre site is beginning to give promise of rare charm and beauty. The new buildings are almost completed. The foundations are laid for the $100,000 chapel. One-half the cost of the twenty-five buildings has come from Burma, the other half from America. Though the money for these has come in the last few years, they may be looked upon as the fruit of Adoniram Judson's own labors. The Judson Fund, through which most of the American money came, caught its chief inspiration from a desire to perpetuate this College, a memorial to the great missionary. In like manner the gift of the churches of Burma, covering one-half the cost of the chapel, was a thank-offering for the one who might well be considered their founder. Yet there is another, a peculiar sense, in which Judson's own hands might be said to have laid brick on brick as these buildings took form and comeliness. Sixty per cent. of America's share in faculty houses, classrooms, and dormitories, and all its share in the chapel came from a single benefactor. The usual channels to Baptists' largest giver had closed. Then the hand of the Master himself seemed to touch the strings of memory. Many years ago when Adoniram Judson was on furlough, a mother had taken her son to meet the great missionary. The memory of that sainted mother and of the touch of Judson's hand worn with suffering for Christ in Burma, brought an eager offer to meet the entire balance of the cost. And more, there was added a challenge to Burma Baptists. Dollar for dollar would be given toward the proposed chapel. So Judson's own hand touched a heart, and the continuance of Judson College was assured.

In 1813 Adoniram Judson found in Rangoon only one rude mission house and a missionary's grave. Today in the same city he would find a tremendous center of activity and a college which worthily bears his honored name.

[NOTE. "Questions for Discussion," p. 159.]

II

VOYAGES AND MOTIVES

Kitna dur hai?—" How far is it? "—was the first phrase
learned by the writer when on a hike in Hindustan.
That question mastered, a search began for "yards,"
" rods," " miles," that the answer to it might be understood. Disgust ensued, for there were no words for
linear measurement in the *Handy Manual for Beginners
in Hindustani.* Just for practise sake, however, he tried
Bhimpore kitna dur hai?—" How far is it to Bhimpore? "
—on the next person met. The reply was a profound
salaam, a pointing to the third quarter of the heavens,
and an *Uster may, Sahib*—that is, the arrival at Bhimpore
will be when the sun reaches " Over there, sir."

After all, the reply to *Burma kitna dur hai?* is more
accurate in terms of time than in the miles which place
it just half-way round the world from America. The
schedule for 1931 for most missionaries is six weeks
from New York to Rangoon via London or Liverpool,
though it is possible to make it a week less by crossing
France by rail. If a traveler does not mind the high cost
he can cover the distance in twenty days provided he takes
the British Air Mail in its seven days series of "hops"
from Croydon, England, to Karachi in Northwest India.

Vinton Voyages

Leslie Mae Seagrave, great-great-granddaughter of the
first Vinton, may find it possible (see map) by 1944 to

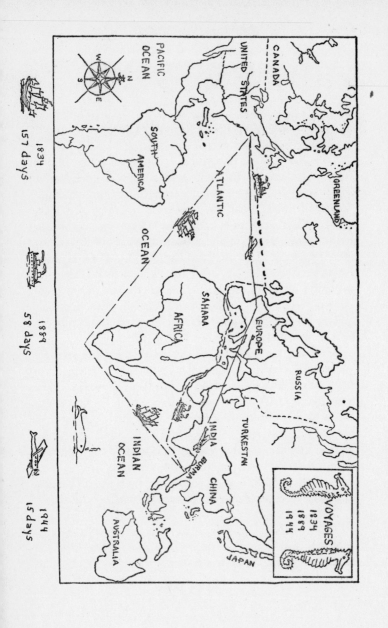

return to Burma by airplane in fifteen days. Her grandmother, Alice Vinton Seagrave, has made various voyages by steamer via the Suez Canal in six weeks. Justus Hatch Vinton himself, the head of the distinguished Burma branch of that well-known family, made his first voyage by sailing ship. Of this trip a very different tale is told both as to time and also as to the trials of travel. May we then take a few bits from the log of the Cashmere and get a picture all too typical of travel conditions a century ago. The Cashmere made the first direct missionary journey Boston to Burma, by the Cape of Good Hope. She was an old-fashioned barque hewn from the Maine forests by farmers, of " ship rig, with a square stern, a billet head, two decks, and three masts." The passenger list consisted of sixteen missionaries, among them Jonathan Wade, chief chronicler of the voyage, and Justus Hatch Vinton, preeminent in the unbroken service record of his family through almost a century; 1931 finds the Vintons represented not only in Rangoon but also in Moulmein and Namkham. Delve then into the old records (those yellow pages of the days when all s's were f's, and where a writer describing the missionary convention as a " beautiful sight," has by his typography made it, for modern eyes, a " beautiful fight "), find there the account of their historic trip to Burma as sent home for publication and signed by the seven missionary men of that party. It is full of descriptions of study, of " religious exercises," of monthly " concerts of prayer," of members of the crew " forgiven and accepted by the Saviour," and it closes with the statement that those days on shipboard had been the " happiest portion of our lives thus far." To all appearances, sea travel was simple in 1834.

VOYAGES AND MOTIVES

The searcher was not satisfied that this report told the whole story. Calista Vinton says her father was seasick for six weeks. That certainly is not the time for the adjective " happiest." A further investigation into the files found certain old letters of a century ago. Among them was a journal—a report not intended for publication. It begins in November, 1834, and is signed " J. Wade." In this document there is " confided to the disposal " of the Foreign Secretary some interesting items regarding those one hundred and fifty-seven days on the high seas.

The Cashmere Voyage in 1834

When the first entry is made, after four months and a half at sea, fresh provisions have become a matter of major importance and Jonathan Wade records:

You know I made an effort to get the live stock increased, and the result was the addition of six pigs. It was thought by you that the supply would give us fresh meat two days in the week all the passage. I did not expect this, nor have we realized it. We have had but one meal of fowls during the voyage (the rest of the fowls were cooked occasionally for the sick). When a sheep was killed, it afforded us a single meal in a week, that is a fresh dinner on Sunday. When we had a pig, it would furnish a meal also for Monday. But *ten of the pigs died,* and why? Because they were put in a pen far too small for the number. Eighteen pigs were put in a pen five feet six inches in length and four feet six inches in breadth, and nearly half of that room was taken up by the bow of the long boat. They absolutely had not room to stand, much less to lie down, and the consequence was they died off until they were reduced in number proportionately to the size of the place in which they were confined.

Lack of fresh meat was somewhat made up by plenty of fresh bread made of flour or meal.

[17]

We have had no cheese for many weeks and no ham. Out of the five hundred pounds of ham put up we have only had a little for breakfast, not more than thirty times, I should say, during the voyage. There has been great waste on it on account of its being so fat, also that the mice got in and devoured much of it.

November 24: All of our stock is now gone except one old chick. Sugar and molasses are running very low. The last barrel of flour has been broached. We were forbidden fresh water for washing our teeth, but the next day the Lord opened the windows of heaven and poured out such a supply that we have not been reduced to that extremity since.

A great source of distress for those deeply devout folk was the rude, irreligious attitude of certain members of the crew, particularly the supercargo and the clerk. These two, becoming " inflamed with wine," took to ridiculing

sacred things, getting up the dog or cat and talking to them about religion in a way that would show how much contempt they felt for the suggestions which had been offered to them to induce them to think of their souls. One evening they got into a high strain of ridicule on the words, " While Shepherds Watched Their Flocks by Night," turning the words into lasciviousness, drinking toasts to the missionaries either collectively or individually, denominating them by the term of brother or sister with the addition of some remark to give a point to the toast, or following it with an attempt to sing some song, though I feel thankful neither of them are singers.

Such incidents might seem humorous but for the thought of the more than twenty-two weeks in those exceedingly cramped quarters. The vessel was a small one. The Port of Boston Certificate of Registry, No. 194, describes it as having " length 115 feet 3 inches, breadth 27 feet 8 inches, depth 13 feet 3 inches, and tonnage 397–46/95 tons." To the sixteen missionaries confined in space so limited, these daily annoyances must have at times been irritating almost beyond endurance.

By December 3 the lack of vegetables and fruit was beginning to have most serious consequences; the record reads:

Still at sea and our circumstances are becoming truly alarming. Four of the men are laid by with the scurvy, and the disease is making sweeping work. Some others of the men are scarcely able to keep up. Our cook is among the number of those laid by. The steward is complaining of the symptoms of the incipient stage of the disease, so are three of the officers (though they are ashamed to own the fact) and the greater part or at least half of the passengers are in the same state, some of whom have been complaining for the last two or three weeks.

December 4: Had what I should call a mutiny on board this morning. The captain laid violent hands on one of the men. He resisted, and the captain called the officers, and the men called the crew. The passengers now left the deck. It was a scene of great anxiety, but there was no further violence. We are entirely out of sugar and have broached the last cask of water.

Already forty days late, no one knew whether the breeze would hold; if it did they should reach Burma soon, if not the crew would soon be helpless. All faced death. Then December 6 brings the joyful entry, in a hand already grown stronger: " Today arrived at Amherst." The journey ended, its hardships forgotten, it soon became " the happiest portion of their lives so far."

Frontier Stations Today

" How far is Burma? " For Vinton and Wade the answer is 157 days full of the things that try men's souls. Justus Vinton and Jonathan Wade accepted Christ's word " uttermost " as an absolute imperative. Few have gone farther, in days and weeks, for anything than they did for Christ. Yet even today long, time-consuming journeys are by no means eliminated. Howard Malcolm in his *Travels* in 1836 took three weeks from Rangoon to Ava, near Mandalay. That journey can now be made in great comfort between noon of one day and six in the morning of the next. Yet there are still stations which may be truly said to be on the frontier—Haka and Namkham— each about a week from Rangoon and still involving slow and tiresome transport. Kengtung, till 1914, was as far from Rangoon by travel time as New York. It now takes almost half that time. Sandoway and Tavoy are still isolated towns inaccessible by rail. Contact of missionary with missionary is difficult. Some have even today a real taste of that loneliness that would have driven mad less courageous souls than those of a century ago.

Missionary Motives: 1. A Vital Experience

What could possibly have induced men to go so far and endure so much as did those pioneers? Why do able men and women today follow in their train? Motives are difficult to know of a certainty. Common judgment would certainly discover radical differences in dynamic between 1813 and 1931. Without question the main theme of today's message is more that all mankind may have the " fruits of belief " than that they may secure the means of escape from the " fruits of unbelief." Yet the perusal of old letters and a reading of present-day missionary candidate papers will carry the conviction that the compelling motives back of the missionary movement have not radically changed through a dozen decades. Modern youth is much more likely to find himself tangled in a

maze of new phrases. He finds it difficult to state in
"rational" terms why he wishes to answer the call of the
East. The youth of a century ago, on the other hand,
slipped on, as it were, a garment which his professors had
already cut for him. Finding satisfying phrasing was
much simpler, therefore, then than today. The marvel
of the humble South Indian outcastes being manifestly
gripped by Christ is often the subject of comment. It
would seem the much more marvelous thing that Christ
can find his way through the mass of knowledge with
which modern youth is overwhelmed and secure a like
manifest control of his life. In most colleges during the
greater part of the first century of the American Foreign Mission enterprise, the ministerial student followed
a very limited curriculum to attain a quite adequate grasp
of the main outlines of human knowledge. The prospective theolog today dips into a dozen fields of knowledge
any one of which might well take a lifetime to master.
He proceeds just far enough to be crammed with queries.
The wonder is that the Light does penetrate through this
mass of ideas much undigested, that Christ does grip
college men and women with a compelling experience and
send them out to the uttermost parts of the world. Without question the first great motive impelling both nineteenth and twentieth century missionaries is such a vital
experience of the power of Jesus Christ.

Missionary Motives: 2. The Needy World

Second of the main motives is the call of a needy world.
It is, one may fairly believe, a misapprehension as to this
need that makes modern youth hesitate before the definite
answer, "I will go, send me." We, today, know vastly

more of foreign lands than was true in the time of Judson. Yet the very mass of the knowledge tends to prevent a real grasp of the whole truth. The modern college youth sees in his University " Cosmopolitan Club " a group of young people from foreign lands of exceptional ability and promise. There is not so often the realization that these are only a selected few. They are tremendous in potential power for molding the future of their father-lands. But they are such a small minority as to face grave danger that their flaming idealism may be smoth-ered under the great mass of age-old lethargy. They all too often find themselves upon return separated by a great gulf from the vast bulk of their countrymen. In the task of bridging this gulf, they warmly welcome assis-tance from America. U San Ba, Burma's voice in *A Call for Colleagues* (1929), cries, " Come over here to wear out your life and to lose yourself among the people, and you will be rewarded in seeing yourself built up in the nations that are being born." East and West are now working shoulder to shoulder to solve some of the great and appalling problems. In this joint task there is no place for self-superiority. There is not, and must not be, however, any lessening in the sense of the superiority of the Message. Only that can empower one to " lose himself."

Missionary Motives: 3. The Great Commission

Third among the main motives should be placed the command of Christ. Here it may be said is the greatest contrast between " the chosen few " of old and the larger group of today. " Commands today are not the mode and will simply cause rebellion." One must, it is urged, reason with modern youth. Yet any student of psychology knows that a word whispered at the right moment can win as immediate action as the command, more or less stentorian, of our grandfathers. Christ's " Go ye " may then have thundered from heaven; today it more often is a " still small voice." It still wins quick and whole-souled action.

"Loyalty to God and Christ, love to man, the tremendous want constrain us " today. They have constrained men from the days of the apostle Paul down. They make foreign missions " the most Christian aspect of the Christian program." It in a peculiar sense above all other parts of that program demands unselfishness. One would not for a moment deny this statement so far as Judson was concerned. One could not have much of self-interest left in his system after a thirty-two year " first term of service " in the Burma of his day. To see those who " follow in his train " today sail on a trans-Atlantic liner may make it seem an attractive adventure. And yet sometimes one wonders whether these days which distinctly demand that the missionary shall " decrease " while the Nationals " increase " are not more than ever exacting in unselfishness. It is much easier to head an enterprise able to act and to command action than to be a partner giving oneself mainly to making oneself dispensable. The great granddaughter of Justus H. Vinton, Rachel Seagrave, who heads the splendid Karen High School in Rangoon, has in many ways a much more difficult task than did the distinguished pioneer. Motives must be of the highest, the mandate of the Master must be supreme if the modern foreign missionary is to continue long his task. Yet how superb the task, how marvelous the opportunity, if one but knows Christ and can bring men to him.

BAPTISTS IN BURMA

Burma's Mission Stations

These motives have sent Baptist missionaries into many parts of Burma. The wide variety of races, languages, and dialects has made their work exceedingly complex. Let us make an aerial survey, seeing the stations and some of this complexity. Taking off from Calcutta we swing due east across the many mouths of the Ganges River. Just across the border of Burma, high up in the Chin Hills are Haka and Tiddin. As we turn to the south down the Arakan Yomas, every valley of this western backbone of Burma adds *Chins* with a different dialect. It is three hundred miles, however, before we see off at the left on the west bank of the Irrawaddy our next Chin station, Thayetmyo. Some eighty miles southwest of Thayetmyo is Sandoway. That sounds near, but these two towns are separated by one of the wildest stretches of almost impenetrable jungle one may find anywhere. The Sandoway churches are mostly Chin, but there are multitudes of unreached Burmans. We drop down from our heights into the valley on the east and wing our way across the tip of the Irrawaddy Delta. Here are Bassein, Maubin, and Pyapon. All three minister to both *Burmans* and *Karens*. The delta is dotted with their villages. Striking out across the Gulf of Martaban and pointing our craft southeast by east we soon sight the beautiful beach at Maungmagon and a bit beyond it on the river, Tavoy. Here is some of our oldest work, both Burmese and Karen. As we come back north along the coast-line we see Moulmein. This city has churches for Burmese, Karens, *Talaings, Indians,* and *Anglo-Indians.* Separate schools for each of these races except the Talaings have been necessary. Before the British captured Rangoon this was the great center for Baptist work. Great things are still being done there. But haste is necessary. To the northwest is Pegu in the midst of rice-fields, dotted with hundreds of Burmese villages. Up the Sittang River valley are Nyaunglebin and Shwegyin; these together with Toungoo reach back up into the hills to the east to help the Karens. The Burmese folk of this area are divided between Pegu and Toungoo for their shepherding. One only needs to note the number of villages with Buddhist monasteries to realize how overwhelming is their task. One more station is on the Sittang, Pyinmana. It has an agricultural school which is also an evangelizing agency. Turn now sharply east up into some of Burma's most beautiful hills. Here and there you see the steeples of Karen Baptist churches. Sixty miles brings us to Loikaw, the only station in Karenni, the red Karen country. In these steep hills live also the long-necked *Padaungs*. Thirty pounds of brass make their striking neck adornment which is ten inches high. The Shan States are just north of us now. There are stations at Mongnai and Taunggyi, with Kengtung far to the east and Namkham far to the north. The swift-flowing Salween River is our guiding line between the two. On these hills and high plateaus are found four races, the *Shans, Taungthus, Lahus,* and *Was*. From these last have been the greater ingatherings. Work for them extends to Bana and Meng Meng beyond Burma's border. At Namkham we come into the Kachin country. Bhamo to the northwest and Myitkyina north of it are also stations for *Kachins*. Our later visit to this country will be one of our most interesting.

BAPTISTS IN BURMA

From Myitkyina we drop rapidly down the defiles of the Irrawaddy. Bhamo is again sighted, then far to the south we see Mandalay and its sister city, Sagaing. Nor must we forget high in the hills to the east, the summer capital, Maymyo. It is the center of activity for a group of missionaries and a place of escape from the heat of the plains for many more. Swinging on a detour through the dry belt we pass Meiktila, back to the river again and we are over Myingyan. Far below it Prome is passed. All these six are Burmese stations. Myingyan High School and evangelistic work are entirely in charge of Burmese Baptists. Below Prome in the rich and densely populated delta, before we descend onto the Maidan at Rangoon, we have four stations. These are Henzada with outstanding work for both Burmans and Karens. Thonze and near-by Tharrawaddy are closely linked, the same praise must be meted out to them. Last of all we pass over Insein. The Burmese Women's Bible School and the two seminaries, Burmese and Karen, mark it as a center of first importance.

Many of these places will see us again. Each and every one has a story worth telling. One impression, at least must not be forgotten. Within Burma's boundaries, due to racial differences, are at least nine different missions. In literature, in training of leaders, and in adequate care for the work, this has increased the complexity of the task far more than ninefold.

III

FOUR ESSENTIALS

Francis Mason's Hobby

By-products of Bible translation sometimes startle. At the same time they indicate the magnitude of the task. For example:

> Burmah: Its People and Natural Productions, with Systematic Catalogues of the Known Mammals, Birds, Fish, Reptiles, Insects, Mollusks, Crustaceans, Annelids, Radiates, Plants, and Minerals with Vernacular Names. By Rev. F. Mason

This octavo volume of 913 pages " owes its origin to the wants experienced " by the translator of the Bible into Sgaw Karen. There are " between seven and eight hundred names of natural productions " in the Old and New Testaments. The author thought, " How much more lucid and interesting will appear the Book of God if these terms be rightly translated." So the collection of notes became a hobby. Often, " to forget weariness when traveling, when it had been necessary to bivouac in the jungles, while the Karens have been seeking fuel for their night fires or angling for their suppers in the streams," the author " occupied himself with analyzing the flowers or examining the fish or an occasional reptile, insect, or bird that attracted attention." These notes he codified into a book, still an authority.

All this was just an incident in the labors of that rare

linguistic genius, Francis Mason, one of many missionaries who have striven to untangle the varied tongues found in Burma.

Essentials of Success: 1. A Mastery of the Mother Tongue

Adoniram and Ann Hasseltine Judson are, of course, America's trail-blazers in the learning of an Asiatic tongue for the purpose of preaching Christ. The Judson journals draw a vivid picture of this " first formidable " undertaking of the missionary. The acquiring, as adults, of an Oriental tongue is a terrific task for most foreigners. They have passed the age for easily twisting their tongues about new tones unknown in English. Too, the work for which the missionary has come cries for action. Many a missionary today goes to a field with a large Christian community still looking to him for advice in all decisions of major importance. Then, too, in a large number of places the leading Nationals understand English. Compelled at first to depend on this English, the pressure is strong for this dependence to become a habit. The missionary's effectiveness is certain to be crippled thereby. It is rarely possible for one of the West to win one of the East to the Master except by the channel of that man's mother tongue. This is not simply because one's own language holds guard over one's own heart, but because language study has many by-products. It adds much knowledge of the " habits, prejudices, customs, courtesies, proprieties, religious tenets, superstitions, and natural tastes of the people." One cannot convert without an understanding of these basic elements so vitally affecting the religious attitudes.

[28]

FOUR ESSENTIALS

An Oriental Attitude

A question in the Judson College registration blank called for the name of the mother as well as that of the father, for there are no family names. Daw Zun is the capable mother of Saya Tun Pe's fine family. That mother's name was often given with reluctance. Yet it was in no sense due to any feminine inferiority in the household. The Burmese mother occupies a large place in the hearts of her sons, yet mention of her name is not made with the ease of the West. Such reticence must be understood if one's approach is to be well received. The path one must travel to acquire the language and the power for effective phrasing of one's message is a long and tortuous one.

The Judsons' Sixteen-Hour Day

The modern missionary in many fields has an excellent language school. This is a tremendous help in surmounting this first great barrier to effectiveness. Burma has never had such a school. The twentieth-century student of Burmese has books and English-speaking teachers. Still he often must laboriously extract such knowledge as he can from one who knows nothing about teaching methods. The task today is simple, however, compared with that undertaken against almost overwhelming odds by the first missionaries. The Judson letters of their first four years, 1813-1817, in particular, are crowded with comments on efforts put forth to master Burmese. " Nancy," as she signs herself in a letter to a friend, pictures a typical day. This is the routine faithfully followed, not for a few days only, but for many weary weeks and months during the early years:

We rise at six in the morning, commence study at seven, breakfast at eight and after breakfast have family worship. We then go to our study and attend to the language closely, till half-past one, when we dine. We generally exercise for half an hour after dinner, then attend to our study again till near sunset, when we take a walk, either out among the natives or in our verandah; take tea at dark, after which we have family worship, then study till ten, at which hour we retire. I go to bed feeling as much fatigued as any farmer can after a hard day's work. I find it no easy thing to acquire a foreign language; and though our teacher says we gain rapidly, yet we can hardly perceive that we make any advance. It is a most beautiful, easy language to write, but very difficult to read or pronounce.

With the help of palm-leaf manuscripts Felix Carey of the English Baptist Mission had made some progress. He gave them the beginnings of a grammar and dictionary. The Portuguese Catholics had made a start on translation work but it was " too Romish." Judson on a blistering April day declares:

I have been here a year and a half and so extremely difficult is the language—perhaps the most difficult to a foreigner of any on the face of the earth, next to the Chinese—that I find myself very inadequate to communicate divine truth intelligently. I have, in some instances, been so happy as to secure the attention, and in some degree to interest the feelings, of those who heard me; but I am not acquainted with a single instance in which any permanent impression has been produced.

An artist has painted a picture of the great translator with slender hands fingering the leaves of the Burmese Bible while the face is uplifted, glorified. " Nancy " gives a more intimate portrait. " Could you look into a large open room which we call a verandah, you would see Mr. Judson bent over his table covered with Burman books, with his teacher at his side; a venerable-looking man in his sixtieth year, with a cloth wrapped around his middle and a handkerchief round his head." It is the month of September, so add a humidity through which only grim determination can carry on. Catch as well the reference to his teacher's garb or lack of it, not forgetting that with Buddhist benevolence, the learned " saya " must shoo away, not kill, the mosquitoes which continually alight on trousers rather open to attack since they consist simply of tatoo.

Difficulties Any Student Meets

After two years and a half at this task Judson had begun to form certain convictions. They are worth quoting, for they ably express modern experience:

I just now begin to see my way forward in this language, and hope that two or three years more will make it somewhat familiar; but I have met with difficulties that I had no idea of before I entered on the work. For an American to acquire a living Oriental language, root and branch, and make it his own, is quite a different thing from his acquiring a cognate language of the West or any of the dead languages, as they are studied in the schools. One circumstance may serve to illustrate this. I once had occasion to devote a few months to the study of French. I have now been above two years engaged in the Burman. If I were to choose between a Burman and a French book, to be examined in, without previous study, I should without the least hesitation choose the French. When we take up a Western language, the similarity in the character, in very many terms, in many modes of expression, and in the general structure of the sentences, its being in fair print (a circumstance we hardly think of), and the assistance of grammars, dictionaries, and instructors, render the work comparatively easy. But when we take up a language spoken by a people on the other side of the earth, whose very thoughts run in channels diverse from ours, and whose modes of expression are

[31]

consequently all new; when we find the letters and words all totally destitute of the least resemblance to any language we have ever met with, and these words not fairly divided, and distinguished, as in Western writing, by breaks, and points, and capitals, but run together in one continuous line, a sentence or paragraph seeming to the eye but one long word; when, instead of clear characters on paper, we find only obscure scratches on dried palm leaves strung together, and called a book; when we have no dictionary and no interpreter to explain a single word, and must get something of the language, before we can avail ourselves of the assistance of a native teacher—*Hic opus labor est*. . . It unavoidably takes several years to acquire such a language, in order to converse and write intelligently on the great truths of the gospel. . . A young missionary, who expects to pick up the language in a year or two will probably find that he had not counted the cost. If he should be so fortunate as to obtain a good interpreter, he may be useful by that means. But he will learn, especially if he is in a new place, where the way is not prepared, and no previous ideas communicated, that to qualify himself to communicate divine truth intelligibly, by his voice or pen, is not the work of a year. However, notwithstanding my great incompetency, I am beginning to translate the New Testament, being extremely anxious to get some parts of Scriptures, at least, into an intelligible shape, if for no other purpose than to read, as occasion offers, to the Burmans with whom I meet.

Essentials of Success: 2. Bible Translation

If one should make a road-map of that translation task, it would be unbelievably long and tortuous. There are two long trips up the Irrawaddy to the royal " Golden Presence " at Ava. There is an intended three-months' trip to Arakan for health which a storm at sea changes into a journey, via the Coromandel Coast and Madras, of eight months while Mrs. Judson in Rangoon has no word from her husband. One would find, too, twenty-one months in horrible Burmese jails. That part of the trans-

lation road-map has a thrill all its own.   After many days
of imprisonment filled with intense anxiety Mr. and Mrs.
Judson are finally allowed to meet.

One of the first things Mr. Judson inquired after was the manuscript translation of the New Testament.   Part of it had been
printed, but there was a large portion, together with important
emendations of the printed part, still in manuscript.   Mrs. Judson
had secreted it, with her silver and a few other articles of value,
in the earth under the house.   It was now the rainy season, and
if the paper remained in this place any considerable length of
time, it would be ruined by the mold.   It was thought unsafe to
allow a manuscript of this kind to remain in the house, from
which every article was subject at any moment to be carried away,
as, once examined it would certainly be destroyed.   The final conclusion was to sew the manuscript up in a pillow, so mean in its
appearance, and so hard and uncomfortable withal, that even the
avarice of a Burman would not covet it, while Mr. Judson himself should undertake the guardianship of the treasure.   As he said,
"When people are loaded with chains, and sleep half the time on
a bare board, their senses become so obtuse that they do not know
the difference between a hard pillow and a soft one."

The Burmese Bible in Prison

Such an arrangement safely guarded the precious manuscript for several months.   Then one day a band of men
rushed into the prison yard.   Some seized the white prisoners, and added two more pair of fetters to the three they
already wore.   Others snatched up pillows and mattresses,
and whatever other articles came within their reach.
Stripped of their few comforts the prisoners were uncere-
moniously thrust into the inner prison.   "Night came, but
brought with it no rest . . . Judson recollected . . . some
passages in his translation capable of a better rendering."

While Judson lay wondering as to the fate of the old

pillow, the jailer was trying to use it as a rest for his own head. Finally he tossed it aside with disgust, wondering at the odd taste of the white man. So it lay neglected till the day the prisoners were driven through the hot sands from Ava to Aung Binlay. Then one of the ruffians ripped open the mat covering the precious pillow and threw away the apparently worthless roll of hard cotton. The next day, that devoted disciple, Moung Ing, stumbled upon this relic of the vanished prisoners and carried it home as a memento. Not till several months later was the manuscript found within uninjured. It is now a part of the Burmese Bible which Judson was twenty-one years completing.

Unwritten Languages

With all its difficulties Burmese did have its written tongue and its large manuscript literature. Sgaw Karen, on the other hand, had neither. To Jonathan Wade fell the elusive task of catching " the fleeting breath of Karen speech " and reducing it to writing. He used the rounded characters of a modified Burmese alphabet. This work required great zeal and scholarly ability. More than one Baptist missionary in Burma has had a like difficult task.

Essentials of Success: 3. The Printed Page

The urge behind all this work of translation is easily understood. Through the printed page one could " speak " in hundreds of places to which he could not possibly go. This was, and is, particularly true among the Burmans. The Buddhist monastery is always the best building in any Burman village. Located in an attractive grove, the monk was always, and still is in many places, the schoolmaster. No village can be found without those able to read. Such reading is almost invariably aloud, and any one who wishes may come and listen. It is in this way that in recent years the Nationalist Movement has stirred even the remotest Burmese villages with a desire for independence. Every Burmese village boy is taught in the monastery schools long passages of Pali, the language of the Buddhist writings. Burmans from the beginning continually asked if there were such " sacred books " written about the " Jesus religion." No country between Europe and Japan offers anything like as large a percentage of readers. That means of preparing the way for Christ to enter into Buddhist hearts is by no means being employed as much as it should be. Much has been done. Much remains to be done.

Burma's Many Translators

The many languages found in Burma and the need of at least " the New Testament, the charter of the Christian church," in each has inevitably divided effort. One might almost surmise that Burma was the original site of the Tower of Babel. Scripture translation has been done by Burma missionaries in more than eight languages. Each has required effort almost equal to that of the Judsons. The Bible has been completed by Francis Mason in Sgaw Karen; by D. L. Brayton in Pwo Karen; by J. N. Cushing in Shan; and by Ola Hanson in Kachin. The New Testament was translated by J. M. Haswell into Talaing and by Herbert Cope into Chin. Many others have made a contribution to the Christian literature of Burma. Some real progress has been made toward histories, harmonies, and commentaries. Three veteran missionaries, H. H.

Tilbe, J. McGuire, and E. N. Harris, are now devoting their time to literature. There are four papers printed at the Mission Press: *The Morning Star* and *The Tavoy Shepherd* in Karen, *The Messenger* and *The Harvest Field* in Burmese. The last is published by the Christian Literature Society for Burma. It has also published recently, among others, *The Life of Booker Washington* and *Little Black Sambo* in Burmese. Yet a great field remains, and one must agree with a modern translator "that the man who can produce Christian literature that grips the reading public of Burma may do more than any other to bring them to Christ."

The New Testament's Premier Place

In this literature the New Testament, of course, takes first place. An axiom of foreign missions is that the missionary cannot evangelize the world. He plants the first seed and wins the first converts. He helps form these into churches. He depends on the churches to become the main means of spreading the gospel. To such churches the message of the Master in their own tongue is an indispensable guide.

That method, too, is least likely to confuse Christianity with Western civilization. Such confusion must be carefully avoided today. Experience of what has actually come from the West to the East, calling itself civilization, enables one to enter somewhat into Mahatma Gandhi's feeling. He calls it " black art " and would banish it bag and baggage.

By that method may the East find more harmony than the West has as yet succeeded in securing! Many mission fields have representatives of only one American church. Burma is in large part a Baptist land. It should all have been, but little can be said where others have come to take what Baptists failed to occupy. This has, however, now and then led to clashes, than which there are few greater hindrances to the acceptance of Christ.

A Question the Bible Does Not Decide

The New Testament in the mother tongue as seen through Eastern eyes does not, however, solve all problems. There is, for example, no direct authoritative decree as to the price to be paid for wives. But let Herbert Cope of Tiddim, Chin Hills, tell his own story:

Because of the division of the Chins into almost innumerable tribes and dialects it is impossible to pass resolutions at the Associations which deal with customs and relations of Christians thereto. We have thus developed regional gatherings where the particular tribal customs are discussed and regulations adopted. There resolutions are not the kind one hears of at the Associational or Convention gatherings, but they are real attempts to coordinate Christianity and the social customs. Social and religious customs are like scrambled eggs—it is almost impossible to separate them.

I have just been to one such meeting. It is the first tribe in which there were Christians and yet after all these years we have not settled on how certain customs will be treated by the Christians. We sat through two long days talking and conferring and in the end had to postpone three of the most important matters until next year. The opinion was so divided it was useless trying to pass a resolution. For instance, what should be the dowry paid for a wife? The system is as old as the Chins, and the price has been steadily going up until a man asks enough for one daughter to almost keep him the remainder of his life and the young groom goes deeply into debt. The original idea probably was that the father lost the labor of his daughter, and the one who secured it should pay. And that is the reason a number of the Chins marry young; they do not want a wife, their parents want some one to work for them. We have been steadily trying to reduce this dowry. I have not wanted to do away with it altogether. Divorce would then become very prevalent. If the husband is in the wrong he loses the dowry, while the father of the wife, if she is at fault, must repay the full amount. Some of the people were for sixty rupees and some for one hundred, and there they stuck and neither would give way. A few said the custom should be abandoned. Then a preacher was called on to give the Scriptural teachings on the matter, and to my surprise he found some passages. The only trouble was he misinterpreted them in a way which would make a professor scream. I did not know what to do, so, as in all such cases, did nothing but awaited events. Finally a small committee was appointed from the various groups. Then I had to do something, and suggested that since there were so many ideas and opinions it would perhaps be better to let the matter rest over until next year, and all joyfully assented. In the meantime I can set the preacher straight.

The first essential for effective service is, therefore, a mastery of the language of the land. The second is the translation, at least, of the Bible. The third is printing. Fortunately the American Baptist Mission Press is prepared to print, and is capable of printing, any worthy work. Its output includes many different languages.

An Oriental Alphabet

On October 15, 1816, George and Phœbe Hough, a printing-press—just a hand affair—and a font of Burmese type secured at Serampore, arrived in Rangoon. A full font of Burmese type is something fearfully and wonderfully made. The Burmese alphabet has thirty-two consonants, ten vowels, and two diphthongs—simple enough so far. It is when you get to the combination of these that trouble begins. Four of these consonants may be combined with many other consonants, singly or doubly, and with different combinations among themselves. In addition all the vowels may be combined with each of these consonant combinations. And each of these combinations means a new character in the modern Burmese font. K-y-o, to illustrate, is not printed as three letters but that combination becomes a new character. The Burmese compositor has two cases with six hundred and seventy-five different sorts of type. How to devise a linotype which could handle these was a problem which taxed the master mind of Frank Denison Phinney. A linotype for English work was easily adapted to the Chin and Kachin which use Roman type but slightly accented. As for Burmese the arrangement finally used was to put three hundred and sixty, the most common characters, at the command of the operator of the keyboard. All the rest must be picked up from side cases and placed in position by hand. The Lord's Prayer is printed with only two turnings to these side cases which indicates how successfully the difficult problem has been solved.

A Fine Mission Press

Since 1904 the American Baptist Mission Press has been housed in a fine building of its own on Merchant Street, Rangoon. It is " the handmaid of the whole mission on the business side of its endeavors." Its educational and commercial printing is large and now carries the entire overhead. It is possible, therefore, to print religious literature economically. It can as well assure for the Scriptures that high degree of accuracy which is essential. Its work has won it a high place among the mission presses of Asia. Of recent years, through colporters, it has made a major contribution to the evangelistic work of the mission.

Essentials of Success: 4. Trained Colleagues

So have progressed Bible translation and printing. But what of the spoken word? In the early eighteen-forties, about a decade before the second Burmese war, the Eleventh Triennial Convention met in Philadelphia. It appointed a committee to consider " the expediency of the establishment of the Karen Theological Seminary at Moulmein." This resulted in a call to a prominent pastor in Savannah, Georgia, Joseph G. Binney, to go to Moulmein, to take charge of pastor training for the Karens.

The pageant, " The Redemption of a Nation," written by Dr. and Mrs. H. I. Marshall, captivated the Burma Baptist Convention in Moulmein in 1928. It paints a vivid picture of the century of Christian Missions among the Karens. In it, the Recorder cries:

Leaders were needed. Men trained in the sacred lore, who should teach them all things that He had commanded. For four-score years the Seminary has been their teacher, sending out her sons both far and near both to teach and to preach, to pastor and to evangelize. Not yet have they finished the fight. Though thousands have been won to the new-found Book and its Saviour, yet multitudes are still with old customs content and ancient tabus still abound. Up, my men, the task is yours, and the victory awaits your attack.

Students and Curriculum—1847 and Today

Picture the four who responded to that call, " Up, my men," to form the first graduating class of Newton, not in Massachusetts, but in Obo, just north of Moulmein, Burma. This class of 1847 were: Phrahai, whose " peculiarity is that he preaches with great point and power to the heart and to the conscience "; Kyahpah, a man who has manifested a deep interest " in all that affects the welfare of the churches "; Aupaw, " Tried in the fire of persecution and pronounced to be pure gold "; and Tahoo, a man who has " too much attachment to the plain, simple gospel as he first learned it ever to go astray." Such were the type that Binney found when he came to Burma. Who could wish for better men! Yet they were but diamonds decidedly in the rough; magnificent material, but with almost no previous schooling. In that regard after four-score years one finds a striking contrast. Take a recent entering class as they gather at the Karen Seminary, now at Insein, twelves miles north of Rangoon. One can only sense the tremendous difference when he realizes that the great Karen church has followed along, step by step, with the advance in the training of its ministry. This entering class numbers thirty-three; a goodly number of them are high-school students; all have had seven or more years of schooling—sufficient to place them in a position of leadership, while not weaning them away from the village churches.

Another contrast is in curriculum. That used with a little group in Tavoy may perhaps be taken as typical of what Binney found. It included: " Reading and writing—for of all things the Bible must be made intelligible. Arithmetic with some Plane Geometry and Geology, Land Surveying with practical lessons measuring the Mission Compound. The Karens must learn to protect their land. Materia Medica in its bare rudiments. A monthly original composition in their mother tongue and a monthly sermon to be preached and criticized." And besides all these " Their principal study was theology, with the Bible as their text-book." The whole of the New Testament was studied verse by verse. Effort was made to render historical and other allusions intelligible—a large task. All practical passages were brought home to the conscience of the students and the attempt was made to make " the lecture-room a Bethel and every lesson a sermon."

Place over against this the courses offered today. The Bible is still the center, but built about it there is a strong, well-balanced three years' course of study comparable to America's best Bible schools. This includes a finely planned and ably directed course in field evangelism. Week-end campaigns and subsequent conference have marked an advance in meeting modern conditions. There is also offered, to qualified high-school or college graduates, a full course of four years in English, with its B. Th. or B. D. degrees. This last department is conducted in cooperation with the fine Burmese Seminary located on the same compound. The Burmese Seminary has not only trained many men for work among the Burmans. It has served all races except the Sgaw Karen. Its last graduating class spoke seven mother tongues. It has trained leaders for the far frontier hills as well as for the Irrawaddy valley. These two seminaries, supported in large part locally, are playing a great part in winning the ruby—Burma—for the King's crown.

Seminary Equipment

Today there is on Seminary Hill at Insein a spacious compound. Both Burmese and Karens have good buildings here. Both are ably staffed. Winding up on the Karen side is a laterite road bordered by beautiful rows of trees. At the top on the right stands the main building, a large, attractive teak structure, combining chapel and classrooms.

Across from it are the two Mission residences. One finds, too, the Haskell Gymnasium and a dining-hall, and best of all two new brick buildings—units of the Daniel Appleton White Smith Memorial recently erected with half the cost met from Karen gifts. In these fine, two-story buildings are housed over a hundred students. Altogether this will make, when the houses for the Karen faculty are completed, a fine plant.

Visit any one of the 977 Karen churches, 957 self-supporting, and one is almost certain to find the pastor a graduate of this Seminary. The leaders who have made possible the magnificent equipment at Bassein, the fine and rapidly growing group of buildings at Henzada, the Morrow Memorial rising in Tavoy, as well as the great advance steps in the Rangoon, Moulmein, and other fields, have many of them been men who passed through those Seminary halls. Many, too, have gone to the frontiers, some even across the border into Siam and China.

Two Recent Graduates

Just two among many of recent graduates may be mentioned: Thra Sein Nyo with his young wife are up in the Triangle, two weeks' journey beyond Myitkyina. This, until recently, was a wild piece of unadministered territory. Then Government released four thousand Kachin slaves. Among these the two Karen missionaries are at work. Another, B. Tha Ya, is the son and grandson of Nyaunglebin pastors. In 1929 he returned to that promising field as a seller of books, a starter of libraries, and a personal worker of unusual ability. He has opened doors in many villages. Meeting a man on a path to a rice-field he begins the story of salvation. He strives to answer the query of how Christ's way is better than Buddha's. The story is not completed when the rice-field is reached. He tucks up his *longgye* and descends into the mud and water. As they reset rice plants the message is continued. A friend is made and a future visit will be welcomed.

Foremost in all that the Karen Seminary has accomplished, memory brings four faces: Dr. and Mrs. D. A. W. Smith and Dr. and Mrs. W. F. Thomas. The message of these two Christian homes on the Hill was one of the finest contributions to the Karens.

Such is the tale of four great essentials of Kingdom advance anywhere—missionaries who are masters of the language of the land, the message translated into the mother tongue of the people, that message so multiplied in print as to be easily placed in the hands of any interested, and fourth, pastors, intimately acquainted with the thinking of their own people, trained to interpret that message.

IV

CERTAIN BARRIERS

A Bit from Boardman's Experience

One day, late in July, 1827, George Dana Boardman, his wife and little Sarah Ann, were walking on the road that led from the first Mission compound in Moulmein to the Thayagong Bazaar on the Salween River, three blocks below. There soon followed them more than sixty little folk from the near-by Burman houses. To our eyes, Boardman is the fine type of American found frequently among the volunteers for service overseas. His features are clear cut, with something of sternness in his countenance; tall, spare, a bit Lincolnesque of figure; gait firm and moderate, bending a little forward, sometimes his chin rests on his chest; forehead high, " but inclining in direction backward "; large blue eyes deeply set under a projecting brow—a man twice looked at anywhere. First scholar of the first class of Colby College—America has produced no finer specimen of manhood.

Yet to the bright black eyes of these sixty Burmese youngsters he appeared, simply an odd, somewhat distorted, pale copy of their elders. And in the minds of those elders, watching him with curious eyes as they sat cross-legged on the tiny front verandas of their high-perched bamboo houses, he was evidently connected with the Red Coats of His Majesty's Forty-fifth Regiment, stationed in the cantonment, a mile away; for, as one of them said, they " look alike, talk alike, are alike."

Eighteen months before there had been concluded the Treaty of Yandabo. Its terms included the cession to Great Britain of the rich Brahmaputra Valley of Assam, the east coast-line of the Bay of Bengal, including Arracan and Tenasserim, together with Martaban east of the Salween River. In addition, an indemnity of one crore (ten million rupees) had been demanded; of which twenty-five lakhs (two and a half millions) had been paid. Awaiting the second instalment, the British army still occupied Rangoon. That the Burmans should joyfully accept one who was inevitably associated in their minds with such imperialism, is just too much to expect of human nature. Boardman records that they "at first . . . endeavored to silence me by sneering, laughing, and jesting, but being filled with compassion for their souls, I spoke freely of Christ's suffering and death and a future judgment. At length they became silent and attentive. Was never so badly used while exhibiting truth and never felt so much pleasure in suffering reproach for Jesus' sake."

From the Karens, on the other hand, in their villages hidden in the jungle, away from the main lines of travel, Boardman could not possibly have received a warmer welcome. "They showed us all the kindness in their power, bringing us presents of fowls, ducks' eggs, yams, fish, plantains, various sorts of rice, and everything which the village could furnish."

Buddhism Is a Chief Barrier

Why this striking contrast in attitude on the part of the two peoples of the same country? The reasons were many: Among them must be reckoned the difference in religion. Yet that other reason—the effect of the British invasion—can by no means be overlooked. Certainly Burmese Buddhism stands out in startling contrast to the animism of the Karens. No enterprise is more easily criticized than one ten thousand miles away. The most common objects to which the correctors of the mission cause direct their attention are the missionary and his methods. Neither is perfect. When all has been said, however, the outstanding factor is all too often forgotten. The chief reason Christianity has not swept the world is: Mankind everywhere has firmly fixed religious attitudes. They are already set in paths other than those pointed out by Christ. Another faith already fills the mind, grips the emotions, and directs the life in certain very definite forms of conduct. No matter how much a missionary may vow " the smoking flax he will not quench," it remains that most of these attitudes must be changed.

These attitudes, the chief hindrance to the advance of the missionary enterprise, are peculiarly present among Burmese Buddhists. They have a religion that advances considerable claims to being of all religions the most logical. It is a strong social force. Through festivals and the ever-present yellow-robed priest it penetrates every corner of the daily life. From its hold it is well-nigh impossible to free oneself.

The Three Objects of Worship

At the center of this religion for the Burman is the story of Buddha, the Law, and the Sangha. No Westerner can help but be stirred as he sees " The Light of Asia " through the eyes of Sir Edwin Arnold. The Prince Siddartha, the Buddha-to-be, is seeking soul-peace; Sir Edwin paints him as with

His tearful eyes raised to the stars, and lips
Close-set with purpose of prodigious love.
He cries: "Farewell, friends!
While life is good to give, I give, and go
To seek deliverance and that unknown Light!"

Yet Arnold paints a picture unquestionably colored by his own Christian training. Turn then to what Bishop Bigandet calls "The Legend of the Burmese Buddha," believed by his followers in the land where Buddhism is found in its purest form, to be a true account of his life. In his invocation the Burmese narrator chants:

I ADORE Buddha who has gloriously emerged from the bottomless whirlpool of endless existence, who has extinguished the burning fire of anger and other passions, who has opened and illumined the fathomless abyss of dark ignorance, and who is the greatest and most excellent of all beings.

I ADORE the Law which the most excellent Buddha has published, which is infinitely high and incomparably profound, exceedingly acceptable, and most earnestly wished-for by Nats and men, capable to wipe off the stains of concupiscence and is immutable.

I ADORE the Assembly of the Perfect, of the pure and illustrious Ariahs in their eight sublime states, who have overcome all the passions that torment other mortals, by eradicating the very root of concupiscence, and who are famous above all other beings.

A Bit from the Buddhist New Testament

There follows Gautama's life-story. Believe this legend, and the "I adore" is understandable. The "Payalaung," the god-to-be, was born in northern India in the sixth century before Christ. A Crown Prince of the Kapilawot country on the very day of his birth, he "freed himself from the hands of those attending upon him, and stood in a firm and erect position on the ground . . .; conscious of his superiority he jumped off the distance of seven lengths of a foot." Attended with like wonders was every event of this, his last mortal existence. In spite of all the luxury of the royal life, of three palaces each nine stories high, and of the forty thousand maidens devoted to his amusement, the future Buddha was dissatisfied. On a certain day he rode forth in his beautiful carriage, richly caparisoned, drawn by four horses. By the side of the road was the form of an old man " the body bending forward, with gray hairs, a shriveled skin, and leaning languidly on a heavy staff "; his first glimpse of old age. Another day, on his way to his garden, " a sick man appeared quite sinking under the weight of the most loathsome disease "; his first sight of sickness. On a third occasion, there came the knowledge of death when the shocking sight of a corpse first met his eyes. When to these three experiences was added his first glimpse of the meek form of a monk, the " prince felt instantaneously an almost irresistible inclination to embrace that attractive mode of life."

A short time later the climax came: It appeared to him that his magnificent apartments were filled not with beautiful maidens but " with most loathsome and putrid carcasses." His determination crystallized. He called for his horse, Kantika, which " felt an inexpressible joy at being selected for such a good journey and testified his joy by loud neighs, but by the power of the Nats, the sound of his voice was silenced," so that the king, who might have prevented the departure, was not disturbed. With one last glance at his new-born son, Raoula, he departed, determined to become a Buddha.

"His progress through the country resembled a splendid, triumphant ovation. Sixty thousand Nats marched in front of him, an equal number followed him, and as many surrounded him on his right and on his left." Finally, on the banks of the Anauma River, the prince divested himself of his royal garb, donning in its place the simple yellow robe of the monk. Then, with one hand he unsheathed his sword; "with the other, seizing his comely hairs, he cut them with a single stroke." Throwing them up into the air, "they remained suspended in the air until a Nat came with a rich basket, put them therein, and carried them to the seat of Tawadeintha." Suspending from his neck the bag containing the earthen begging-bowl, he departed in search of enlightenment.

Six years were spent in meditation, at the end of which the Payalaung undertook a great fast, allowing himself only the use of a grain of rice or sesame a day; finally denying himself even that " feeble pittance," he eventually fainted, fell on the ground, and was thought by many to be dead. Upon recovery from the swoon, there swept over him the uselessness of fasting and mortification. He, therefore, refreshed himself and withdrew into the forest for further meditation. Finally, "a little before break of day in the hundred and third year of the Eatzana Era, on the day of the full moon of Katson, the perfect science broke at once over him. He became the Buddha," the adored one.

The Four High Roads of Buddhism

First the prince, then the ascetic, then the enlightened one, he is a figure fine enough to grip the imagination of any people. As a fitting climax add the preacher of the

four great truths of the Law " that can dispel ignorance "
so " the coming out from the whirlpool of existences can
be perfectly effected." These four truths are: "Afflictions
and miseries attend the existence of all beings. Passions
and, in particular, concupiscence, anger, and ignorance,
are the causes of all miseries. Neibban, the exemption
of all passions, is the deliverance from all miseries. There
are four high roads which lead to Neibban." To pass
through these one must leave the world, renounce all
pleasures, practise patience, study the law, and meditate.
If these things are done, " The four roads to perfection
are opened before him. These he must follow with per-
severance; they will conduct him to Neibban. They are
a perfect belief, a perfect reflection, a perfect use of
speech, and a perfect conduct." This Law, very logical,
fascinates the intellectually inclined among the Burmese
people.

A Modern Buddhist Monk

As to the Assembly: Take a modern picture, that of
the monk of a monastery in a bit of a grove beside the
Irrawaddy on the road to Mandalay. The old Pongyee
with his robe of yellow—the color of dirty rags—and his
shaven head—his hair, the great source of vanity, gone—
sat on the unwalled first floor, away from the heat of the
March noonday. I was waiting for the Flotilla steamer
down to Prome. He greeted me with a kindly smile, a
freshly spread mat, and all the gracious hospitality typical
of the Burmese. An order sent a bit of an *upazin* scurry-
ing up a near-by palm-tree, and soon there were refresh-
ments of fresh cocoanut milk and cakes. Christianity and
Buddhism were discussed for an hour and more. To my

query he replied: " No, I will not attain to Neibban this Pawa. It will be many existences yet before perfection." So every question is answered with a gentle tolerance. What more natural than that the villagers should venerate this lovable old gentleman, striving to live in the spirit of the Buddha as a toiler on the Fourfold Path.

So much for the Buddha, the Law, and the Assembly— the objects of adoration of every Buddhist. All are tinged with pessimism. The East Indian living in poverty and hunger finds in them a future filled with gloom and foreboding. The true Buddhist should be " a world-weary philosopher." Yet it is not so with the Burman. In a land with ever-abundant rains and so comparative prosperity, his " Kan," or fate, becomes just luck. He, a born gambler, wagers his last rupee that it will be good. Buddhism, pessimistic in theory, in actual practise has become bound up with all the national festivals. The Burman makes it a thing of gaiety, a happy-go-lucky philosophy of life, " with funerals no less festive than marriages." Till old age compels it, he refuses to face his sin and its punishment. Therein lies a great difficulty in converting him to Christianity.

The Christian Message to Burmese Buddhists

What then is the Christian message to Burmese Buddhists? The qualifying adjective—Burmese—should be carefully noted; for " four hundred and seventy millions of our race live and die in the tenets of Gautama, and the spiritual dominions of this ancient teacher extend, at the present time, from Nepaul and Ceylon over the whole of the Eastern Peninsula to China, Japan, Tibet, Central Asia, Siberia, and even Swedish Lapland." The varying

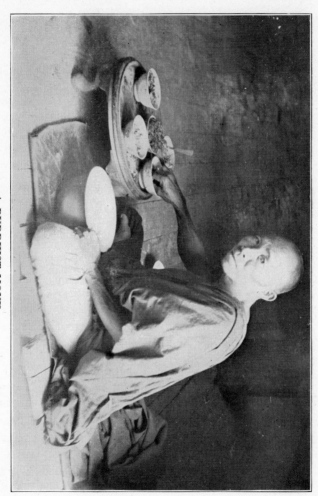

A BUDDHIST MONK

Pongyee at Nyeindama Eating Midday Meal

climates and cultures have inevitably created a wide range of Buddhist faiths. Then, too, Christian-trained critical scholars of its sacred books have brought forth still further interpretations, Christian and otherwise. So into these various branches of Buddhism has crept a wide variety of teaching. It is to be feared that Gautama Buddha himself would not recognize many of his commandments either as now chanted in Eastern monasteries or as preached in Western pulpits. This infinite variety must inevitably affect the Christian approach.

One may say the missionary " simply carries Christ " to Burma. Yet, as I sit in my study on Lower Kemmendine Road, Rangoon, a thousand, perhaps many more, pass daily, each almost without exception bent on securing simply his own selfish, sordid ends. Against that background, peak points in the Christian message must appear. While Christ and Gautama are both historical characters, the Buddha is hidden by " the mist of legend that envelops him," while the account of Christ has the ring of fact. Gautama " was a pure, noble, true man." The missionary who bears a merely human Jesus has no message for Burma. The Buddha set standards of conduct much higher than those of his day. Any added heights are futile unless with them comes the Living Son of God to help. This Living One is to lead to the Father. They two will break the Buddhist wheel of weighing merit, that balancing of one's good deeds against the bad which haunts many a devout Buddhist elder. The Burmese proverb says, *ku-tho t'be, a-ku-tho t'bait-tha*—merit a trifle, demerit a ton. In other words, it is hopelessly impossible to pile up sufficient merit to outweigh one's demerit. The Buddhist monk alone leads an " ideal " life.

Yet even he cannot break the bonds of his evil deeds. To the Buddhist it seems unbelievable that there is One who gives life more abundant both in this world and the next— One who releases from the treadmill of seeking one's own salvation. Can it be that unselfish service for others is this world's greatest good? Can one by forgetting self best prepare for the life to come?

Buddha's Self-sacrifice

The "birth stories" tell of the Buddha's various existences—One gives a glimpse of the sort of self-sacrifice found in Buddhism. Read it as written in *The Light of Asia*. Gautama meets a starving tigress and her two cubs:

> "And how can love lose doing of its kind
> Even to the uttermost?" So saying Buddha
> Silently laid aside sandals and staff,
> His sacred thread, turban and cloth, and came
> Forth from behind the milk-bush on the sand,
> Saying, "Ho! mother, here is meat for thee!"
> Whereat the perishing beast yelped hoarse and shrill,
> Sprang from her cubs, and hurling to the earth
> That willing victim, had her feast of him
> With all the crooked daggers of her claws
> Rending his flesh, and all her yellow fangs
> Bathed in his blood: the great cat's burning breath
> Mixed with the last sigh of such fearless love.

Such tales to the modern mind seem too fantastic to be true. In power to stir one's heart they are separated by æons from the story of the Cross. The Bearer of that supreme symbol of self-sacrifice is every day lifting the load of sin. By him men are daily empowered to enter on paths of service. This is the message. Yet if one is to understand at all the missionary task, he must see through this account how Gautama captures the imagination and fascinates the intellect of many millions.

Buddhism a Greater Barrier than Animism

As over against this Burmese belief in Buddhism, the Karens were a primitive people, never sufficiently developed to embody their ideas in literature. To them the essential part of religion was not belief, but practise. Their primary aim was to avert the anger and secure the aid of the supernatural beings that lurk not only in the animals, but also in the trees, rocks, springs, plants, weapons, and heavenly bodies—spirits of all sorts; weak, powerful, kind, unkind, helpful, and hurtful.

In theory the two—Burmese Buddhism and Karen Animism or spirit worship, a view of life better seen when we travel " Beyond Mandalay " among the Kachins— stand at the opposite poles among non-Christian beliefs. In actual practise Buddhism is itself mixed with animism, yet the Burmese Buddhist, with his literature and lofty ethics, naturally finds more mental hazards on his path to Christ than does the animistic Karen largely dominated by blind fear.

Mother Burma

Then, too, the Karens, driven hither and yon, had no country they could call their own. Hunted as if they were wild beasts, they could easily accept alien help. On the other hand, no man has a more beautiful fatherland than the Burman. Stand beside the old Moulmein pagoda looking eastward upon one of the world's most beautiful bits of scenery—a valley of striking charm: In the foreground are trees of every hue, the dark olive of the mango, the

light green of the pagoda-tree, the graceful plumes of the
bamboo. Over the trees, a mile away, the Salween spreads
out into a magnificent sheet of water, studded with green
islands, with glistening pagodas and monasteries; to the
east, beyond the Attaran, rise isolated, fantastically shaped
ridges of limestone, in part bare, elsewhere with jagged
peaks partially concealed by straggling clumps of vegeta-
tion; off to the south, the dark Taungwaing Hills, their
somber color relieved only by more glistening white
pagodas. India's farthermost province is often entranc-
ingly lovely. National feeling, religious emotion, and love
of beautiful " Mother Burma " are inextricably inter-
woven in the mind of the Burman. That which disturbs
one, threatens all, and is deeply resented.

Red Coats and Religion

The Karens not only accepted Christ in great numbers;
they, driven beyond endurance by Burmese persecution,
also bore arms for the British. Trained to stalk the
beasts of the jungle, they turned that talent to the aid of
the alien invaders. They live today in separate villages,
with comparatively few contacts with the Burmese. So the
years of British rule have seldom seen occasion for strife
between the Burmese and their fairer skinned neighbors,
the Karens. Yet a wireless message from Rangoon early
in 1931 tells of a petty revolt led by one Shwe Kyi Lone,
" the only Golden Crow." This " King of Dragons," by
an offer to tattoo " bullet-proof " charms, won some one
thousand two hundred followers and set himself to estab-
lish a " Burmese Buddhist Kingdom." Though the royal
edict names Englishmen only as enemies, he is reported to
have burned two Karen villages, " because the Karens are

loyal to Government." So even today in some places the fires of hatred are smoldering. This is true though decades have passed since the Karens rendered their outstanding service and won the sobriquet, " Loyal Karens." No one would question but that they took a natural course. By this conduct, however, they undoubtedly built barriers for Christianity's advance among the Burmans.

So it was not alone the difference in religion that made the Karen more responsive to the appeal of Christianity. The fact is that in the minds of Burma's peoples the white face, whether British or American, whether magistrate or missionary, was inevitably associated with British military men. Their Red Coats meant to the Karen relief from oppression. Those same Red Coats meant to the Burman the passing of his fatherland into the hands of the British Bureaucracy. At best, a conqueror rarely wins the hearts of the conquered, and the religion of the conqueror rarely wins ready acceptance from those among his subjects who at one time belonged to the ruling class.

To the missionary writers of the early days, the conquest by the English was a source of intense gratification. The intolerance of the Burman powers to all except the national religion was now broken. The East India Company would no longer feel bound by its agreement to protect heathenism. There would be toleration for the new religion. So the missionaries rejoiced in the success of the British arms as " an answer to prayer." If the prayer was with the hope that this success of the British arms might lead to success in winning Buddhist Burmans, then that hope is even to this day to a large degree unrealized. The major mission problem still is, how to lead to Christ the many millions of Buddha's disciples.

Karen Traditions and Ko Tha Byu

One must never forget another—a positive and powerful factor in bringing the Karens to Christ, namely, the religious traditions of the people which included the story of "The Book of Silver and Gold" and the "Y'wa" legend which also played a tremendous part. This last tells of the placing of the first parents in the garden by "Y'wa," the Creator; "their temptation by a dragon to eat of the forbidden fruit," and continues with a creation story closely resembling that of the ancient Hebrews.

This legend has exercised a strong influence upon the Karen people. To be sure, it did not supplant the ancient animism of the tribes any more than Buddhism has displaced spirit-worship among the Burmese. Nevertheless, it was accompanied by the prophecy of the return of the white brother with the Lost Book, which inspired the Karen with the hope of a better future and furnished an admirable foundation on which Christian teachers could build in promoting the development of the Karen nation.

Such was the setting for Christian conquest among the Karens which awaited the coming of the missionary who should call an apostle from among their own people.

On May 16, 1828, in Tavoy, Boardman "repaired early in the morning to a neighboring tank and administered Christian baptism to Ko Tha Byu, the Karen Christian who accompanied us from Moulmein." Such is Boardman's simple record of what must be looked upon as the great event of his short missionary career—the baptism of the first Karen convert; for Ko Tha Byu was destined to become a member of that group of whom Christ said, "Greater things than these shall ye do." Uncouth and unlettered, but literally aflame with the glorious gospel,

CERTAIN BARRIERS

Ko Tha Byu went through the hills and valleys from Mergui to Sandoway, unmindful of personal hardship, indifferent to exposure, summoning the Karens. This people prepared by traditions listened eagerly to the apostle's message. He promised the fulfilment of their long-deferred hope. He gave a glimpse, not for a moment to be forgotten, of a future—perhaps here, certain hereafter —free from oppression. From the seed he sowed there sprang during his own brief life a church of more than a thousand members. They have become the great Karen Baptist community reckoned today as almost 180,000.

Some Favorable Factors Today

No like progress has been made among the Burmans. Yet a most hopeful factor for the future of the Kingdom is the changing attitude of the Burmans toward the Karens. The " national schools " of recent years founded, supported, and managed by the Burmans, have brought to a large group of ardent patriots a practical lesson in the difficulties and expense involved in education. With this has come, too, a real respect for the notable achievements of the Karens. A Minister of Education, a Burmese Buddhist, declared that the Bassein Karen schools would be the theme of his addresses everywhere. Parliamentary experience has more than once proved the sound wisdom of the Karen representatives in the Legislative Council. Even more promising, Karen College and Seminary men have gone with gospel teams to Burmese Mission Schools and found an effective message though given in their " second language." All these are elements of a new day in Burma.

Another factor not so often mentioned, but by no means

to be ignored, is the able Karens in government service. They are rendering outstanding service. Among these is Saw Bee—an Oriental name any American can pronounce. Trained in interracial contacts at Judson College, he was appointed a " D. I. S."—a Deputy Inspector of Karen Schools. His first assignment was the fertile delta district of the Irrawaddy. Well built and of gentlemanly bearing, he shows as good taste in dress as any Burmese. He, therefore, moved most acceptably whether in conference with the District School Board or among the villages. The majority of the villages were Burmese. All the members of the District Board were Burmese Buddhists. They naturally felt that all schools should close on the Buddhist sabbaths. There are four of these " Ooboat-nays " in the lunar month. They vary in date with the waxing and the waning of the moon. Failure to follow this rule should mean no payment of school grants. The Karen villages of that district are many of them Christian. Karen Christians observe a " blue law " Sunday. Elders have been known to protest against the picking of a flower. To them there was no choice of sabbaths and the loss of grants would be a very severe hardship. Saw Bee went to the Board and suggested a very simple solution. The Board was quite right in insisting that all schools have a six-day week. But might not each local group of elders decide which day should be the " holy day "? That simple solution required the highest diplomacy in its presentation. Racial feeling might easily have arisen. Instead, friendly relations were built up between the two races. Another step was taken toward the removal of a barrier which has stood between many a Burman Buddhist and the acceptance of Christ.

[60]

V

COCOANUT CREEK KARENS

A Missionary Meeting in 1841

The rendezvous was Megezzin; eighty miles south of
Sandoway for Elisha Abbott, forty miles northwest of
Bassein for Shway Weing, the young chief—apparently
within easy distance, but—

Abbott left at ten in the evening on December 23, 1841,
in a small, sharp built, fifteen-ton schooner, a two-master
with fore-and-aft rig, loaned by T. Morton, Esq., Senior
Assistant Commissioner of Arakan. From the deck of the
little boat tossed by the Bay of Bengal, that coast province
presented " one continuous succession of broken, irregu-
lar hills, covered with jungle; apparently one vast howling
wilderness." The Yomas, rising from eight to twelve thousand feet far away on the sky-line, reared their majestic
heads over dark masses of clouds. The villages, if any,
were hidden in the forests along the banks of the mountain streams. Often the foot-hills extended right to the
shore, sending out rocky points a mile or more into the
bay—no simple coast to navigate. Any level land was for
the most part covered with mangroves. At high tide the
salt water flooded in, making marshes from which arose
" a miasma impregnated with fever, cholera, and death."

Into this region Abbott planned to penetrate. For such
a place Shway Weing left the beautiful, gravelly hillocks
of the eastern—the Bassein-side of those same Yomas—
hillocks with thrifty gardens of pineapples, shaded by jack

and mango trees in great numbers; hillocks between which rice grew luxuriantly, and "if the rice crops should fail, the fruit gardens still remain, a land richly blessed of heaven."

Abbott anchored at the mouth of Megezzin Creek at dusk on Christmas Day. At sunrise, in a small dugout canoe of the country, he went for three hours up the stream, past the Burmese village, between banks covered with trees in full blossom, with foliage of all the shades imaginable. It was typical, tropical jungle, the home of "peacocks, tigers, elephants, and gigantic serpents." Not often for Abbott, never for "The Young Chief," was travel so easy. All too frequently, the missionary journey led "over mountains and rocks, through swamps and mud, past the tracks of wild elephant; creeping under trees which had fallen and grown across the path; such a road as it is impossible to give any conception of." Often if it had not been for the hard sandy beach or the mountain creeks, Abbott did not see how he could have made his way from village to village.

But there was no sandy beach nor mountain stream for Shway Weing and his companions as they made their way to the rendezvous. Cowering in their homes under the oppression of the Burmese officials, fearing death at the hands of these same officials, if it were known that they were leaving Burmese territory, these Karens could not go by any beaten path. They must force their way through wherever the thorn-covered mass offered an opening, shivering in the penetrating cold of the jungle night, panting in the intense steamy heat of tropical noonday. After eleven days of wandering, often at the point of exhaustion, they finally covered the sixty miles to their destination.

COCOANUT CREEK KARENS

And the reason for this rendezvous? It is found in the pages of an old journal. On the 30th, the record reads, " baptized ten in the morning "; the 31st, " baptized thirteen, all lived in this village "; January 2, 1842, " baptized eleven in the morning. After morning service on Sunday the 3rd baptized nineteen." It was not until Monday the 4th that Shway Weing arrived, bringing with him others who were baptized at noon in " our Jordan, a small stream running down from the mountains, overlooked by scenery wild and beautiful, the distant forests resounding with sounds of praise from a hundred happy converts."

The Cost to the Missionaries

Try to reckon the cost, the cost of carrying the gospel and the cost of accepting Christ in Arakan in the eighteen-forties. This missionary accounting may be found in an old Annual.

It may almost be said that Arracan's shores are lined with the graves of the fallen, whose memory can never die. Here labored and died the faithful Comstock and his companion, and his remains quietly repose beneath an humble tomb at Akyab—*hers* with two children at Ramree. Sandoway is marked by the graves of Mrs. Abbott and children. At Kyouk Phyoo rests the sleeping dust of br. and sr. Hall, and of br. Campbell. In the Mission grave-yard at Akyab also have been buried the mortal remains of the last Mrs. Moore and of Mrs. Knapp.

The missionary mortality of that day in Burma seems to stand second only to the record of Africa's west coast.

The Price Paid by the Karens

For the cost to the Karens take five scenes from an imaginary drama of Cocoanut Creek.

[63]

BAPTISTS IN BURMA

PROLOGUE: Desiring freedom to worship God, and finding no rest from the Burman oppressor in the Bassein District, Karens cross the mountains to the sandy soil and sickly climate of Arracan. There under the British Raj they need not fear death for reading the Bible.

SCENE I.   JANUARY 15, 1842

Abbott anchors his boat in the small bay at the mouth of Ong Kyoung—Cocoanut Creek. After an hour's walk, he finds upon a little hill, a short distance from the village, a neat chapel with a pulpit "quite in advance of the age."

SCENE II.   APRIL 16, 1843

One hundred and twenty new Christian families, with two hundred and fifty water buffaloes, have made the long, long trek over the mountains from the Bassein side. The chapel that April Sabbath day cannot contain more than one-fourth of the Assembly. Fruitful fields and rivers abounding in fish have been exchanged for mangrove marshes. Yet that matters little. For in Cocoanut Creek "they may worship God in the open face of day, and not a dog may move his tongue."

SCENE III.   SEPTEMBER 15, 1843

Early morning. A large and beautiful chapel (Early Bamboo-thatch Period), eighty dwelling-houses, looms clicking, everywhere happy activity.

Noonday. Cholera, that dread scourge, broke out in their midst, raged, spread with a fatal rapidity. Panic seized the poor people. Parents caught up their little ones in their arms and fled to the jungle; some crossed back over the mountains; many died in the jungle. The fine village becomes a place of desolation, their chapel a habitation of ants.

SCENE IV.   DECEMBER 18, 1843

Abbott, again in Ong Kyoung; his chronicle records: "I struck the gong, the people came together, and I preached a funeral sermon for one hundred and twenty souls."

COCOANUT CREEK KARENS

The annual preachers' training class gathers in the Cocoanut Creek Chapel. Abbott stands among a group of twelve, the representatives of thirty-six pastors of churches, "the greater number of which are in Burma." All are tried men "who have remained steadfast, immovable." Each face is marked with "intense joy at seeing" Abbott among them again. They "rejoice together and offer to the Lord" as only Karens can "a song of grateful praise."

The Karen Martyrs

Few have endured more than those Karens, pastors and people. Some had been "pierced with swords and spears, severely beaten, suspended by their necks from trees and let down before life is extinct to recover strength for a repetition of the cruel torture." Others had incisions made all over their bodies, then rubbed with salt and tortured to death. Men were dreadfully beaten and bound with iron fetters. Women were placed in a boat, anchored in the middle of the river, with their young children left crying on the shore. Christian chiefs were arraigned, imprisoned, fined for embracing the Christian religion and learning to read. Whole villages stripped of everything, including food, driven to beg their rice, were compelled to work as loathed pagoda slaves. So runs a record with few equals for devotion to Christ and the gospel.

Beginnings in Bassein

On the morning of January 8, 1853, there is read in Bassein the annexation proclamation of the British Government. That proclamation has been given in the three languages of the attentive multitude. As twenty-one guns from the stockade, and as many from the steamer anchored in the near-by stream,

[65]

thundered forth the decree of a mighty nation, what various emotions are awakened in the awestruck crowd! The soldier is elated with thoughts of glory. The haughty Burman hears in those peals the doom of his kingdom and his religion, and trembles. But the long-oppressed Karen hears a voice proclaiming liberty to the captive, freedom to worship God.

Thus began a second period of Bassein mission history. During the first dozen years the missionaries were compelled to live in distant Sandoway. To that side of the mountains pastors came for training, and from that side they returned to win converts and care for churches. With the annexation Bassein itself became the permanent mission center for that district. More intensive training to lift the level of these churches is begun.

A Monastery Becomes a Meeting-Place

Even before the public proclamation of annexation, Elisha Abbott and Henry Van Meter had proceeded to Bassein and taken up "temporary settlement." Outside the high, massive brick wall which extended for nearly a mile along the river was what at first glance seemed "a beautiful grove," but further experience proved it to be full of jungle fevers. In it stood an almost new Buddhist monastery. The yellow-robed monks had fled from this *pongyee kyaung* at the approach of the British forces. Major Roberts, the officer in command, had given it to the missionaries. The building was a timber one, and by demolishing a large monastery in good condition near-by, sufficient material had been secured to divide it into three rooms. These became a chapel thirty by fifty feet, and a room each for Abbott and Van Meter. In this building takes place a significant meeting.

COCOANUT CREEK KARENS

Abbott, in failing health, had been carried ashore on the twenty-first. On the next day the Sabbath, July 22, 1852, he preached twice, to the delight of the Karens, and did not seem the worse for it. After the evening service, "there was a meeting of native preachers, twelve were present. The four ordained preachers—Tway Poh, Mau Yeh, Myat Keh, and Poh Kway—had been appointed a committee to inquire of all the assistants as to their losses during the recent troubles and to present their present needs."

Men Who Are Multiplied Many Times Today

The Karens throughout the years have produced many notable men, not least among these were those gathered that July evening in the Bassein monastery. What a short time before had been a depository for cases of Buddhist books, became the scene of a great forward step in the administration of mission funds. Tway Poh, one of the Committee, had for a number of years been pastor of the Cocoanut Creek Church. A "mild and lovely John" without "an enemy in the world. He has ever been a fair high character and acquired a commanding influence, which, in meekness and love, he consecrates unreservedly to the cause of truth." Mau Yeh, another Committee member, was the oldest of the ordained Karen pastors. He perhaps presents the report from the Committee. One finds him pictured as: unusually large and rather uncouth in his personal appearance, with firm mouth and prominent nose, a man of the jungle, with little education and less of eloquence, yet with a power in his speech, for "there is soul and common sense in all that he says." His turban is but ill arranged; he wears two or three long Karen coats, one over the other, and around his neck is a soiled silk handkerchief knotted at the one end to hold some small change while from the other end dangle his keys. As he stands there, with his face alight, his very presence bears unforgetable witness to the transforming power of the gospel.

Partnership Not Paternalism

The case of each pastor was taken up separately by this Committee and recorded in due form. The result was that that some sixty-five dollars was asked for. "This sum, it must be remembered, is all that they have received for almost two years."

So those pastors gathered that night to hear a report which distributed the pitiful sum of two hundred rupees from America among fifteen of them; men, many of whom had lost all of their possessions through Burmese persecutions. The striking thing, however, is not the amount distributed nor the fact that so little could be of any assistance to them, but that even in 1852 there was developing real leadership among the Karens. Even then the watchword of the Bassein Mission was " partners, not employees." The Jerusalem Conference of 1928 coined a finer phrase for the relation between missionaries and Nationals: " partnership, not paternalism." But Beecher and Abbott, Tway Poh, and Mau Yeh practised the principle three-quarters of a century before.

The Cost of Self-support

The report of that Committee in the Buddhist kyoung also furnishes a glimpse of the beginnings of self-help as attained by the Karens. They have today become the out-

KO THA BYU MEMORIAL HALL, BASSEIN

standing group in this regard among Baptist "younger churches" everywhere. Common comment is, "but conditions among the Karens are different." Conditions today are undoubtedly different among the Karens from those found among most Christian groups in Asia. They are now, but were they in the eighteen-fifties? Few folk have ever had a greater ground for appeal to America for funds. Few missionaries have faced more difficult soil in which to sow the seeds of self-support. Yet it was stressed from the first, even though the substitution of the Karen churches for the mission treasury cost Beecher and Abbott "more anguish of spirit and more hours of controversy and pleading than all the other troubles arising from the forty pastors and five thousand converts put together." Shway Weing, Ko Tha Byu, and their associates were not " secured and held to their work by rupees; they went forth living as the fowls of the heaven in the goodness of God, and through their labors multitudes became obedient to the faith." This meant, for more than one pastor, weeks of weary labor in his own rice-fields to secure for himself " self-support." " In the year of Christ, 1849, the Elders of the Church at Great Rock to teacher Abbott " wrote:

We gave our teacher, Shway Bo, during the year, twelve rupees, eight annas [\$4.50]; sixty baskets of paddy; one hundred viss of dried fish [365 pounds]; fifty viss of salt; a bundle of tobacco, etc. We are very poor, O teacher! [too true] and can do but little. Pray for us, that we may be blessed.

It was no great amount for Thra Shway Bo. It was, however, seed planted, later to bear abundant harvest in sturdy independent truly indigenous churches. The sacrifice of the pioneers has today its rich reward.

Present-day mission policy states that " the paramount aim of the Christian missionary is to lead men everywhere to accept Jesus Christ as Saviour and Master through whom they may find the Father." After that acceptance there arises the urgent need for these believers to band themselves into churches; for upon those churches is largely placed dependence for the further extension of the Kingdom. Church life " inevitably seems to express itself in complete self-government, self-support, and self-propagation." At all stages of mission history it has been natural, therefore, to look upon progress in self-support as convincing evidence of vitality, and the securing of such self-support as one of the main problems of mission administration. The Karen churches must be given high rank in this regard. Without a glimpse of the early days one cannot realize the price paid by the missionaries. Nor must one forget the self-sacrifice of Karen pastors and people.

Some Fruits of Century-Old Seedlings

One might catch the contrast between early years and today by walking through the Ko Tha Byu Memorial in Bassein. Dr. C. A. Nichols, for more than fifty years in this field, has made that building perfect in every detail from its copper-nailed slate shingles to its beautiful pipe-organ made of ten tons of Burma's best teak. Remember all its cost has come from Burma. Other Karen stations are also showing marvelous progress along these same lines. Drop down to Burma's farthest south, Tavoy. On the slab which covers George Dana Boardman's grave read the words : " His epitaph is written in the adjoining forests and in the Christian villages of yonder mountains. Who taught you to abandon the worship of demons? Who raised you from vice to morality? Who brought you the Bible, your Sabbaths, and your words of prayer? Let the reply be his eulogy."

With the questions of that epitaph in mind, attend a meeting of Karens from " the adjoining forests." Let Walter Sutton, their missionary, give their reply:

A big question at our Tavoy-Mergui Karen Association was whether the Karen Christians of the District should entertain the All Burma Baptist Convention and celebrate the centennial of the baptism of Ko Tha Byu, the first Karen convert. Bright and early the morning of February 8, 1928, the Karens filled the *mandat* to vote upon this question. It was feared it was too big a job for Tavoy to undertake. It has never been held in so small a town. The Karens have debts and are erecting a new church and school building which will cost a lakh and a half of rupees (about $50,000). The entertaining of the Convention would cost money. These stern figures caused doubt in the minds of many as to the wisdom of entertaining the Convention. But this was the one hundredth anniversary of Ko Tha Byu's baptism. It happened in Tavoy. It can only be fittingly celebrated in Tavoy. Christians all over Burma are anxious to come here for the celebration. A delegation from the U. S. A. is expected. Because we have never done it before, is not a good and sufficient reason why it should not be done now. It was evident that no one was against it on principle, simply upon debts. After hearing different ones give expression to their opinions the Karens were anxious for a vote. They voted. Unanimously they determined to use what they hope will be their golden opportunity to greet their fellow Christians from all over Burma and some from beyond the seas, and start upon a grander century of work for Jesus to whom they owe everything.

Centennial Celebration Subscriptions

When the vote had settled the question, a motion was made and carried to appoint a committee, to apportion the getting of sufficient food for all the delegates. When the report was read Thra Ah Du asked that there be no grumbling over the requests made by the committee. They had tried to divide everything fairly. Then he began and received intensive hearing as he said, " Tavoy— 20 baskets rice, Mytta 10 baskets rice, Et Et 15 baskets rice." So to village after village until the number of baskets of rice reached 337. Likewise the number of pigs asked for totaled 56. Nine individuals promised ten cows. Each Christian was asked to donate one chicken. Certain villages can secure certain foods better than others because of their location. The villages on the sea are to supply all the dried fish. Where vegetables grow well, vegetables will come from the villages. A few villages right in the heart of the bamboo country will supply the thousands of bamboo needed for the *mandat* and the temporary dining-shed and cook-house. In addition every Christian is asked to give eight annas (16 cents) at least. Those Christians having a monthly salary or a good yearly income are expected to give half a month's salary.

Yet that is not all the story. Our new church and school building, the Morrow Memorial, being constructed at the expense of the Government of Burma and the Karens, each to pay half of the cost, is progressing as fast as the Karens can collect their share of the money. Our money was practically depleted when I went to the Association. I had to know how much the Karens would give and when. The afternoon meeting opened with Scripture and a prayer. Then the President of the Association announced that the session would be devoted to the interest of Morrow Memorial. Thra Tudee was called upon for a short speech. He explained the critical financial condition which the building fund faced. With only Rs. 750 in hand and Rs. 20,300 needed as quickly as possible to carry on the building and prevent what has already been built from being damaged by the next rains, which start in May, it was clear to all that they must hustle with their cash contributions for the building fund. There was not much cash to be had, but every one wanted to know how much cash could be counted upon. They proceeded to find out. The people saw three strange-looking blackboards and some snowy white chalk.

COCOANUT CREEK KARENS

An Elephant Helps Build a School

When the invitation was given to come up and write down the amount of the pledges, all eyes centered upon some of the Karen elders. We wanted to see what they would do. Then some shouted for U Shwe Po to start off, but he did not jump, instead he was looking for a hymn to express his thoughts. He selected, "What Hast Thou Done for Me?" He read it through to the people, and concluded by saying he was going to do something for Him. Turning, he walked up to the blackboard and wrote down Rs. 5,580 (about $1,860). That was grand. The people applauded vigorously. Next they were anxious to see Thra Gwaw Po. He took the chalk and said that he did not have cash but some things he could convert into cash readily and wrote that he would give:

1 elephant (cheap at price)	Rs. 3,000
1 piece of paddy land	2,500
1 water buffalo	40
1 cow	10
1 horse	25
1 goat	5

Rs. 5,580

Again there was an outburst of applause. A procession of faithful pastors filed up the aisles to do their part, and not one person failed to give something. Their gifts ranged from Rs. 20/ to Rs. 300/. One was a pastor who works among non-Christians who give him no aid, and who must grow his own paddy in order to live. He has so little that the Christian Endeavor Societies give him Rs. 60/ (about $20) per year to assist him. That man with face beaming wrote opposite his name Rs. 60/ and said, "I get this much from the Christian Endeavor, and I'll give it to the Morrow Memorial Building Fund." The Karens raised in pledges at this meeting the magnificent sum of Rs. 16,527. It was an amount beyond my dreams. Even if it takes nearly everything they have the Karens propose to erect that new school building in honor of Thra Morrow (Rev. Horatio Morrow) who served them so acceptably for 29 years.

Today there are 611 Karen Baptist schools; 593 of these do not receive a rupee of mission aid. Almost all of them are in villages. In Bassein in addition to the buildings of the Sgaw Karens centering about the new twin-towered Ko Tha Byu Hall one also sees a fine group of Pwo Karen buildings a few blocks away. In Rangoon there are the fine brick buildings, replacing long used teak structures, rising about the impressive Vinton Memorial. To the stories of these Karen stations interesting chapters might be added of Henzada, Maubin, and Tharrawaddy, lying between Rangoon and Bassein; of Moulmein to the south; and of Toungoo, Nyaunglebin, and Shwegyin to the north as well as Loikaw back up in the Hills, the youngest of the Karen fields. No finer record is written anywhere in any mission field than that of the Karens.

VI

BEYOND MANDALAY

The Kachin Jubilee

Only seven days after his arrival in Bhamo, Albert Lyon was stricken. On March 15, 1878, the Burmese Governor, the British resident, Jacob Freiday, the new missionary to the Shans, and Josiah Cushing, the veteran missionary to that same race, followed Lyon's crude casket to a grave outside the stockade. Hopes long deferred for founding a mission beyond Mandalay among the Kachins seemed crushed. For all that was left was a single Karen hidden in the hills.

Yet a half century later, just after the Ides of March, 1927, some seven thousand Kachins, a majority Christians, gathered in Bhamo to celebrate the jubilee of the arrival of Thra S'Peh, the Bassein Karen. That gathering gave due honor to two outstanding figures in the Mission's beginnings—William Henry Roberts and Ola Hanson. With these, if one includes the prospector period, may well be placed three well-known names: Kincaid, Mason, and Cushing.

The First Missionary Journey Beyond Bhamo

Eugenio Kincaid in 1833 went up the Irrawaddy from Rangoon to make a " reentry into the Golden City," Ava. There had been no missionary there since Judson left some seven years before. Four years after this reentry a crazed king and a crumbling government compelled his hasty

[75]

withdrawal to British territory. Before his flight he made the first missionary journey into the regions beyond Mandalay.

A small native boat bound for Bhamo and beyond bore Kincaid up the Irrawaddy from Ava. His ultimate destination was Mogaung, " the most northern city of Burma," in the " Great Sacred Lake region, skirted by a territory crowded with people and abounding in amber and serpentine stone." The up-stream trip took twenty-two days, past mines famed even then for the world's finest pigeon-blood rubies and blue sapphires, mines which in 1929 yielded a $35,000 ruby and a sapphire worth half again that amount. Still on he went through the majestic defiles, and within sight of Ta-roke-yo-bong, the " three heaps of Chinese bones." There forty thousand Chinese soldiers, it is alleged, perished in a single day in a battle with the Burmese. One dusk found him at " Great Rock," residence of the Governor of Monheim Province. That official gave much information about a people called Kachins, ordered a sumptuous dinner, royally entertained Kincaid and his companions, and dispatched them the next day, with gifts of rice, dried fish, and vegetables. Many friendly villages were visited. Calls were made at hundreds of homes. Scores of tracts were distributed. The trip was a typical missionary journey. With it came a vision of advance over the Himalayan foothills to join Burma with Assam, the two to become one great Baptist mission field.

Burmese Banditti Capture Kincaid

A very different tale must be told of the trip back down the Irrawaddy. Civil war had broken out. Numerous bands of armed banditti overran the country. The cry of

UP THE IRRAWADDY IN 1834

"Robbers, robbers," had been so frequently heard that at last at Sa-ban-ago it went unheeded. Then suddenly there was the roar of thirty muskets. "I heard some of the balls whiz past my ears, others struck the boat, and some fell into the water. My boat was surrounded by villainous robbers—more than seventy spears encircled my body, I was completely encased by steel points touching me. But God was with me and sustained my courage." Dragged ashore and placed in the center of a council of banditti, they "decided to behead me at sundown, the time of day when all Burman executions took place."

The sentence of the council was providentially postponed. Kincaid was, however, robbed of the last rag of his clothing, a "strip about a cubit wide" being given him to fasten around his loins. "They then tied me with ropes and led me off under a guard of one hundred and fifty men. After six days and nights full of danger, I found means to escape to the mountains, though for thirteen days, nearly destitute of clothing, exposed almost constantly to a burning sun, sleeping in the open air, and on the ground, and obliged to beg here and there a handful of boiled rice, I was enabled to endure it." In this way the nearly one hundred miles to Ava were covered and Kincaid reached home. So ended the first missionary journey beyond Mandalay, and so suffered another missionary, staking new frontiers for the Kingdom.

Bibles: Shan and Kachin

An attempt to go up the Irrawaddy beyond Mandalay was made in 1867. Josiah N. Cushing and A. Taylor Rose embarked at Rangoon, Bhamo-bound in search of northern Shans. Their flotilla steamer, Arthur Phayre, named for the great civil servant, reached Mandalay just after Christmas. They had a happy audience with King Mindon Min and hired a boat for the venture. Then opposition arose to a trip north. Abandoning the boat, with six pack ponies instead, they set out into the hills to the east toward China. That was a pioneer journey among the southern Shans who call themselves " Tai," and it played its part in paving the way for Cushing's masterly translation of the Bible into that many-toned tongue. The Shans had a written language; the Kachins did not.

Francis Mason, master linguist and translator of the Bible into Sgaw Karen, penetrated the country to the north in 1873. He sought Kachins, kinfolk, he was confident, of his beloved Karens. Thanksgiving Day finds that grand old man in his seventy-fifth year sitting in a Burmese zayat in Bhamo digging out a bit of Kachin grammar and a considerable vocabulary of words. This was his last work. To Mason's manuscript Cushing later made some additions. From these meager beginnings Dr. Ola Hanson completed the reduction of the language to writing. Then through three crowded decades he persisted until the entire Bible was translated into Kachin.

Kachins and Karens

A report of Mason's survey was sent to Bassein. He felt sure that " Bhamo is the earliest bit of solid ground we have on which to found Karen history." He found some striking similarities: " The Kachins carry baskets on their backs, like Karens. The Karen, like the Kachin women, use a very peculiar kind of loom in weaving; and the look of the Kachin women is precisely the same. Like the Karens, the Kachins chew the betel-leaf, and call it *pu-lap*—very near the Karen name *Lipu-la*." Catch that similarity if you can!

The experiences of that trip deeply stirred Mason. His " ready pen " further records:

When I looked up to the range of mountains not ten miles distant, but stretching off to the east far as the eye can reach some six thousand feet high, and marked like a mosaic pavement with the brown patches of Kachin cultivation contrasting with the deep green forest, my heart yearned after these children of the mountains, with none to point out to them the way of salvation.

The Bassein Karens caught Mason's vision. Pastor Bogalay was sent to accompany Cushing, who was making another determined effort to get beyond Mandalay. These two reached Bhamo in 1876. Bogalay, cowed by the " fierce sons of the jungle," left in a week, but Thra S'Peh soon came in his stead. His name should be linked with Lyon, Roberts, and Hanson.

The First Missionary to the Kachins

A letter from Thra S'Peh, this first foreign missionary from America's first foreign mission field, shows that the high courage and devotion of the pioneers had caught among the Karens.

POOMAH, JANUARY 11, 1878.

DEAR TEACHER AND MAMA:

I pity this people very much. They want very much to learn; but at present I am all alone on the mountains among them. Owing to fighting among the Kachins and Burmans, I cannot travel about as freely as I wish. The Burmans have given out that they would massacre all the Kachins from fifteen years old and upwards, and I was a little afraid. Teacher Cushing told me not to fear; if the Burmans attacked one mountain, to flee to the next; and, if they should take all the mountains, to flee into China. I did as he said, and stayed on the mountains. I am all ready to cast in my lot with these poor Kachins, to suffer with them, and to lead them with my whole heart to Christ, as Moses cast in his lot with the children of Israel. Nevertheless, I was attacked with fever three times, but not violently. I am not very strong. Pray for me that I may have strength for my work. I will write you monthly of this work. Do you also write me sometimes, and thus strengthen my heart. Salute all the Bassein pastors for me. Finally may you all experience God's favor.   S'PEH.

Four years later W. H. Roberts baptized the first seven Kachin converts. These were the results of the labors of Thra S'Peh. Many such Karens have gone as missionaries to Burma's far-flung frontier. Their contribution is incalculable.

Animism: A Religion of Fear

Missionaries, American and Karen, found above Bhamo a religion very different from Buddhism. Religion among the Kachins is in a large measure like that of any other primitive people. With no literature, its essential part is not belief, but practise. The primary aim of its rites is to avert the anger of supernatural beings and to secure their aid in the struggle for existence. These spirits are some weak, some powerful; a few kind, many unkind; some helpful, most hurtful; in their midst man is compelled to live. His most important task is the adjustment of his relations with them.

Something of this sort of belief still lingers among the conduct-guiding forces even of civilized nations. Much of it is found in the background of Burmese Buddhism. It is our own superstition many times manifold. Thirteen

[81]

reclined at the "Last Supper" table. This fact makes unrentable and so eliminates the "thirteenth" floor from 152 Madison Avenue, New York City. Such superstitions greatly intensified operate as the motive power behind every act of these primitive hill-men.

Ola Hanson gives as his matured judgment that "the savage is far more religious than his civilized brother. Everything he does can be traced to some religious custom and superstition. In his work or amusement he is always under the shadow of his invisible guardians or tormentors. They follow him as his own shadow from the cradle to the grave."

The Kachins' *nats* or spirits are innumerable, occupying every imaginable place above and below. "They rule the sun, the moon and the sky, dwell on every mountain-top, in every spring and stream. Every waterfall, cave, and precipitous rock has its guardian, as well as every wood, field, and large tree. And to this host is added the particular divinities to whom each village, tribe, or family must pay particular attention."

Trees, rocks, or animals are, however, never worshiped. No images of any kind are ever made. It is the varied and sundry ceremonies conducted by the village priest which go to make up their religious exercises. "This priest is, as a rule, the most intelligent and best-informed man in his community. His duties are clearly defined, and he alone is familiar with the religious language chanted at the sacrificial service."

Visible Evidence of Animism

One cannot travel far in the Kachin country without having their demonology brought forcibly to his attention.

The typical Kachin village is entered by a long, shaded, often picturesque path. On either side of this path are several short, squared posts covered with rude models of weapons, household articles, and ornaments. These are "the things most desired by the community." The providing spirits have their place of abode just beyond, so these pictures constantly remind them of the wishes of their worshipers. These spirit abodes are usually placed under some tall and venerable trees. They are shelf-like structures, and are worshiped by the chief as the representative of the village.

Enter the village and before every house is a similar curious collection of shrines for the supernatural guardians of the family. With these no one may interfere. All are receptacles of various kinds of offerings. These are kept intact as constant reminders to the spirits that they are not forgotten. Within the house, whether that of chief or commoner, above the main fireplace is the sacred corner. In it is yet another altar dedicated to the household gods. Any trespass in this place is keenly resented. It is the tearing down of these various altars which marks the day when the family becomes Christian. This ceremony serves as a severe test of sincerity.

So the Kachin goes with danger dogging every step of life. To quote again from Doctor Hanson's authoritative book:

If soot falls from the roof into food that is being prepared, it is a bad sign. If rats build nests in a grave, the relatives of the interred will be poor. If lightning strikes, the *nat* of thunder must have an offering. If a house burns, if a man is killed by a tiger, the *nat* causing such misfortunes must be placated. By far the greatest number of sacrifices are, however, to secure help in time of illness. Disease, in spite of a healthy climate and a great deal of outdoor life, is very common. The belief that the *nats* alone can help has developed a fatalism in regard to health. They often seem entirely indifferent to pain, but in reality they stand a great deal less than their civilized brothers.

Kachins and Cotton Mather

One of the difficult tasks of the British Raj in India has been to dispense justice without clashing with "religious" customs and belief. The Kachins would have made congenial fellow townsmen of Cotton Mather in Salem, Massachusetts, in 1692. Their "religion" makes it impossible for them to understand why the British law prohibits summary disposal of witches. They are thoroughly convinced that witches are demon-possessed, a real danger demanding drastic measures.

The Origin of Burma's Many Races

Such are some of the characteristics of the Kachins, just one of Burma's many races. That country's multiplicity of peoples might well require a Tower of Babel, a flood, and a tidal wave, if one is to try to explain their origin. The Tower, mayhap, was located in mid-Manchuria, the flood spilled its "Joseph's coat" collection of mankind far and wide in China. It ran over into Burma and swirling down the valleys above and below Bhamo, pushed its vanguard back into the high hills, there to form the Karens, Kachins, Chins, and Padaungs, leaving the Burmese and Talaings to occupy the valleys. As though this diversity were not enough, each high mountain ridge found the intervening valley a sufficient barrier to build up a different dialect—an authority claims forty such for the Chin group alone. To add to all this confusion worse confounded the tidal wave of "Tai" swept up from the stormy South China Sea, a wave that did not spend itself till it had reached the high plateaus of Northeast Burma where the Tai as "Shans" pushed Taungthu, Wa, and Lahu likewise up the hills. They are now dominant there through *sawbwas,* petty princelings, loosely tied together in the Shan States Federation. That same wave swept down the rich Menam River valley where the Tai now rule as Siamese. When these inundations had expended themselves a dozen distinct language groups and almost ten dozen dialects were within what are now Burma's borders. All have become native to the soil like the tropical jungle's prodigal profusion of flora and fauna. This has made the mission task most complex.

Of Chins and Shans, Lahus and Was, Taungthus and Talaings interesting stories might be told. For each race important mission work has been and is being done. The Chins' story has been ably told by Mrs. Arthur Carson's *Pioneer Trails, Trials, and Triumphs.* That their forty dialects mean real differences any one of the six or seven Baptist missionaries to those two hundred and ninety thousand hill people will bear witness.

As for the Shans, they are mostly Buddhists like the Burmans. They seem to excel even that race in slowness of acceptance of Christianity. Here again, as with the Burmans, it must be admitted, workers have not been and are not now sufficient to face the task adequately. There are twelve missionaries, American Baptists and English Wesleyans, for more than a million people. Though hidden in the hills, Chins and Kachins, Lahus and Was have proved more accessible, and so have drawn much of the Mission's strength.

BAPTISTS IN BURMA

Recent Immigrants

The human flood and tidal wave referred to above preceded British rule. Since the arrival of the British Raj, two major peaceful invasions, one of "natives" and the other of Chinese, must be mentioned. The name "native" is a thing of pride when it is "Native of Washington, D. C.," or some other desirable domicile. It has a very different meaning when it is "native of India." Burma has some nine hundred thousand "natives of India," about half of whom are Moslems. Many are wealthy merchants, bankers, brokers, petty traders, and policemen, but most are just coolies. These are clad like Kipling's Gunga Din, with "nothin' much before an' rather less than 'arf of that be'ind." Naturally the name "native" is anathema in Burma. Most of them work on the docks, cook, clean, and do a thousand other useful things. A chief task is to care for the rice crop. That garnered, they more often than not return across the Bay of Bengal mostly to the Madras side till the next harvest. Many, though, have sent for their families and settled on the soil. So all together, the Indian community can muster ten seats in the Legislative Council. Among these Indian immigrants a work worthy of extended mention is being carried on. In Rangoon, Union Hall High School, highly commended by Government inspectors, serves as a center. There are churches, too, such as Bethel Baptist back beyond the Shwe Dagon pagoda among the lowliest of the city's servants. Also the Telugu Church which is under the leadership of their own T. B. Joseph, an outstanding evangelistic preacher. Moulmein has its Mizpah Hall School. Missionaries there, as well as others in Bassein, Prome, and

Mandalay, have done much to further the work so capably carried on for many years by William Fredrick and Hannah Norris Armstrong.

The other peaceful penetration of recent years has come from the East. The coastal provinces of Southeastern China have sent shoemakers, shopkeepers, cabinetmakers, carpenters, contractors, and keepers of pawnshops. Chinese now total one hundred and fifty thousand if one includes with these the *thinbau* of the ships and the *anya* of the north who come overland by caravan from Yunnan. No village can call itself a town until the ubiquitous Chinese comes as the dispenser of short-term loans.

With these penetrations, peaceful and otherwise, have come certain amalgamations to add still other distinct groups. Anglo-Indian and Chino-Burman have played most important rôles in the country's development. This close alliance of China and Burma has been a peculiarly happy combination of kindred races remarkably productive of leaders. As for the Anglo-Indians, they vary as widely as the heredity of the "Anglo" half and as the environment in which they are brought up. Many of them have won high places in every aspect of the life of the country. Mission schools and churches, in particular Immanuel Baptist, Rangoon, and the two English Baptist churches at Moulmein and Maymyo, with their American pastors, have played no small part in making the Anglo-Indians the vital element of the nation which they are. As for the Chino-Burman, he has largely had to look to the Burmese church for Christian instruction. From this group have come such able men as Saya Ah Syoo, pastor of the Moulmein Burmese Baptist Church.

BAPTISTS IN BURMA

New Needs Continually Arise

Such statements give just a fleeting glimpse of the varied folk who now make up that cosmopolitan country—Burma. It is a land which is continually opening new doors for missionary endeavor. North of Myitkyina in "The Triangle" the Burma Government recently ransomed four thousand Kachin slaves. Among them the Kachin Baptist Mission Society would send workers. It is that, in part, which leads them to plan to start a small Bible school, headed by the veteran George Geis, in the hills east of Bhamo. There they would train more workers in addition to those who have completed the course at the Burmese Seminary at Insein. Chester Strait at Haka already has such a school with eyes turned toward the urgent needs in the Chin Hills. It is in the far eastern part of the Shan States and on that same plateau as it becomes a part of Yunnan, China, that the greatest ingatherings have come recently. With them, too, has come the difficult problem of how to give adequate training. This mass movement has not been among the Shans of the valleys but from the Lahus and Was hidden in mountain villages east of Kengtung.

Both Sides of the China Border

About a dozen years ago the veteran William Young turned the work in Kengtung state over to younger hands and pressed into the "regions beyond." What he has met there may be best described in his own words:

From Hsi Ken we went a day's journey on our return trip to a large village called Pang Nai. Three small villages under it were awaiting baptism. An official at Ai Hsoi three hours' march from there had attempted to break down the work. Both last year and this he had sent men to oppose and threaten, but the people stood firm. On February 6, 1925, we baptized the four villages, 331 baptisms. In the afternoon we moved on to Ai Hsoi, where a mob collected as we passed through the village. It had no doubt been instigated by the official over a small post there. He was a raving maniac from rage when we reached his place. He ordered it barred and began beating and kicking our workers. He refused to look at our passports or the Governor's edict insuring protection and religious liberty. He ordered the entrance to his place barred and then ordered the soldiers to get their guns. They were ordered to fire on us. A mob of about 300 to 400 was pressing upon us, brandishing spears and long Wa knives. They kept shooting from the crowd. The soldiers were ordered to fire. They were only about fifteen yards from us. We could hear the click of the hammers as the guns were lowered on us, but not a gun of the soldiers went off. We managed to get out of the enclosure in front of the Post, to a place about fifty yards away where we had expected to camp for the night. After being surrounded for about a half hour by the soldiers and mob, and hundreds of shots fired, some of the mob became ashamed of their actions. Harold and my Chinese interpreter had pleaded with the official to quiet down and restore order. The Wa preachers pleaded with the Wa, and some began to plead for order. Others cried, "Kill them all." We were permitted to move on later. No one was seriously hurt. Our pack animals that had been taken were restored. Some of the mob ran ahead and kept firing from ambush as we went along the road.

An Association in the Bana Field

Then there is an account of an association in 1930. It was held in a small independent District, under neither Chinese nor British rule. The District borders on the territory of the wild head-hunting Was.

We arrived March 1, and were to hold our Association March 5-7. On Sunday, March 2, I sent the ordained native workers

out to the Christian villages of that District. There had been no
baptisms in most of the villages for five years, and many children
had grown to baptismal age. I was working in three villages of
about three hundred houses; as I entered the largest village for
10 a. m. service, I heard shouting and the report of guns in a
wooded section not far from the village. I saw villagers running
with their guns to that spot. A band of about forty head-hunting
Was had attacked six boys who were driving cattle and buffalo
out to pasture. Four of the boys were killed, the other two
narrowly escaped. One received a spear wound in the back. The
other they attempted to behead but struck too high, and as he was
wearing a heavy turban, the knife struck the turban and glanced
off his head. Nearly seven hundred were baptized in that section
in villages that had been largely Christian before. The attendance
at the Association was reported as three thousand four hundred.
The day after the Association closed, several groups of head-
hunting Was came and we preached to them in the chapel. About
twenty new villages were baptized on this tour. Some were asked
to wait as we were short of workers to locate with them as pastors.
The work has been greatly strengthened all along the line.

So Burma furnishes varied problems for missionary
effort. In the valleys of the Irrawaddy and of the Shan
plateau the Burmese and Shans are both Buddhists and
both very slow in accepting Christ. While from the hills
which surround these valleys have come the great groups
who are trying to live the life to which the Master has
called them.

VII

WOMEN'S WORK

The Sightseer

The hurried tourist is "doing" Rangoon. He has seen the Shwe Dagon Pagoda across the Royal Lakes at sunset. He has visited the fascinating night bazaar. In the early morning mists he has gone to a timber-yard with its "eliphints a'pilin' teak." It has been perfect so far. What else remains for the last two of his eighteen hours? For a fitting climax go out Umbrella Lane to the Kemmendine Girls' School. Along the lane you will find a bit of Burmese village life. At its end is an example of Burma's best in the fruits of foreign missions. Nothing finer is found anywhere than the cooperative effort of the women of Burma and of America in the education of girls.

Goal and Methods in Women's Work

The goal of women's foreign missions is "the elevation and Christianization of women and children in foreign lands." The methods employed for the accomplishment of this are "evangelistic, educational, and medical." A very able group of women have gone from America to Burma. An equally remarkable group have responded to their leadership. These two are demonstrating beyond a doubt that all three methods may lead to the same great end. The "A. B. M." girls' schools in Burma hold high rank as educational institutions. Their very atmosphere breathes of a winsome Jesus. They train those already

[91]

Christian. They bring non-Christians to Christ. They demonstrate that education may be a method second to none for extending the Kingdom.

Susan Haswell: Founder of the First School for Girls

"Mama Susie," as the friends of her childhood in Burma called her, must take first rank as a founder of institutions in Moulmein. The English Girls' High School, the Leper Asylum, and the All Burma Orphanage are clearly of her conceiving. It was her urgent appeal which brought to Burma the first woman physician, Ellen Mitchell. So came the inspiration for the Ellen Mitchell Memorial Hospital for women and children. The first institution of her founding was, however, Morton Lane School. Hosea Howard came with Jonathan Wade on the Cashmere in 1834. He conducted for some ten years a boarding-school with a department for girls. About fifteen years later Miss Haswell came back to Burma to join her father, James M., and her brother, James R. She found the intelligent, active Christian women of Moulmein had been pupils in Hosea Howard's school. As for the younger women, they could scarcely read, knew little of God's Word, and had their hearts set on money-making. The convictions she formed bore fruit in her day in Morton Lane. She built the "White House." It was a most attractive building. The upper floor was of teak, the lower plastered with cement. Handsome white pillars ran across the front. There is now a group of five fine buildings equipped to care for some six hundred girls. The staff is exceptional. Its work extends from kindergarten to high and normal school. Morton Lane School for Girls has few equals, East or West.

WOMEN'S WORK

The First Four Girls' Schools

Morton Lane and English High in Moulmein together with Kemmendine in Rangoon have celebrated their jubilees. Mandalay Girls' High and Normal School lacks only a few years of its fiftieth birthday. All of them are well equipped. A number of fine buildings have been erected during the last decade or so. They have sent some of their finest graduates to Judson College. Few college women anywhere can surpass that group in charm and capability. Drawn from all over Burma, they receive training not only in the classroom but also in the life of Benton Hall. Just to mention one or two from the Morton Lane group. Ma Nyein Tha is now the smiling, efficient headmistress of her old school. Ruth Ah Syoo, a daughter of the Moulmein parsonage, is a teacher in the near-by Judson Boys' High School. Ma Mya Yin is a Deputy Inspectress of Schools in the Tennaserim Circle. Ma E Tin is back in the High Department of Morton Lane. She made an unforgetable picture when she presented a bouquet to the Prince of Wales. She also stood highest of all the students in the University of Rangoon in the B. A. examination of her year.

Personal contacts in Sunday-school work bring another pleasing picture—that of the staff of Kemmendine. There was just one little group gathered in the house of an evangelist when the writer first began to take the tram to that crowded suburb. The work did not go too well. House-to-house visiting down the crowded street helped but little. Then Ma Hla May and Ma Nyein May came from Kemmendine. Another house opened its doors, and then a third. Many little folk each week hear of Jesus,

Education Plus

Kemmendine has a strong church which meets in the school. After careful preparation there came a gospel-team chiefly of Judson College students. The campaign continued for two days. At the end an invitation was given. More than seventy, most of them from Buddhist homes, accepted Christ. The school has for years been leading many of its students along the Way. There has been no marked opposition. Times have changed, however. Word of these decisions spread rapidly through that quarter of the city. About eighty girls were taken out of school. Many of the decisions were from the older girls. These girls had been for years in the school. The testing-time only deepened their faith. That was a couple of years ago. Last year a similar effort at Morton Lane led seventy girls to make a public profession of Christ. There resulted a somewhat similar demonstration of opposition in that city. Undaunted, the year 1931 brings a report of plans for a campaign at Mandalay Girls' School.

Such is the spirit which pervades the schools for girls. There are sixteen such schools, most of them of grammar grade, in the Baptist Mission. Such Christian women as Kittie Po Thein, Sgaw Karen, and Eleanor San Tay, Pwo Karen, both head mistresses, make this number possible. These schools are open to all races. Chiefly, however, they meet the demand of Burmese and Shan parents for separate schools for their daughters. To the Karens, on the other hand, coeducation has come to be the accepted system. Of the more than 23,000 pupils in Karen Baptist schools, well over a third are girls, while about half the teachers are women.

WOMEN'S WORK

Sarah Higby: Eminent in Coeducation

As "Mama Susie" Haswell has typified the contribution of American womanhood to the separate schools for girls, so may " Sally Higby," as she signs herself, represent the part played by American women in coeducation. Both of these missionaries were familiar figures to any one who knew the Burma Mission a decade or so ago. Miss Higby was a perfect example of that devotion which has made Karen coeducation remarkable in results. One had but to know her Tharrawaddy boys and girls to see clearly placed upon them the imprint of her life.

After thirty years of active service, though fifty-six years old and sorely crippled, she came to Tharrawaddy and carried on for almost twenty-two years more. Her greatest work was accomplished there. She may well stand with Dr. Ellen Mitchell at the head of the list of Burma Baptist missionaries, twelve of whom have been awarded the " Kaisar-i-Hind Medal for Public Service."

The Place of Burmese Women

Work among the women of Burma has always been peculiarly attractive. For women play a very important part in the life of that land. Let us look a little more closely at the Burmese " better half," the women of the dominant race. *The Rangoon Times* of January 6, 1931, carries a headline, " Ward Headwoman Preserves the Peace." There had been serious clashing between Burmese and Chinese in Lanmadaw Quarter of Rangoon. It threatened to spread to the Bahan Quarter, but Ma Pwa Hmyin, the ward headwoman, made it clear that she would not permit it. The " bad hats " took her at her word. In

[95]

few countries do women occupy a position of greater freedom than in Burma. The maiden may keep a stall in bazaar without it being considered anything derogatory. The young man seeing her there is attracted. Nine o'clock at night is, in Burmese phrase, " courting time." At that hour the duly chaperoned calls are made. Once married, she takes custody of her husband's cash. In bazaar and shop the chief part of buying and selling falls to her lot. All this gives a tolerance and understanding which cannot but impress any one who knows her. In Buddhism, as in other religions, the women throw the weight of their influence against change. Yet they are accessible far above most women of India, and are as well more open-minded and alert.

The place attained by Burmese women might in many respects be considered ideal were it not for the mark left on her by Buddhism—a mark difficult to define yet evident in her countenance. The writer was traveling one day on the road from Pyinmana to Kantha. The party stopped at a little wayside bazaar to buy a bit of warm " jaggery," that district's special brand of peanut candy. That master of the vernacular, Lee Mosier, asked the husband sitting by smoking his cheroot about a certain proverb. " Yes," that husband replied, " woman is better than the female but not than the male dog "; for the philosophy of it is that only the male may attain Nirvana. To be sure, our Burmese friend repeated the proverb with a grin and a chuckle. Yet a close observer cannot escape the conviction that this belief, eating at the feminine heart, has written itself on her countenance. Certainly release from that same soul-cramping factor, as found in Christ, completes a personality hard to excel anywhere.

WOMEN'S WORK

Though Buddhist monastery schools have done much for boys, they have done nothing for girls. Hence the opportunity of the mission school. A like opportunity for the united effort of Christian women has been found in alleviating suffering.

Two Rangoon Physicians

It was late one hot and sultry afternoon in 1923. My thoughts were turning to afternoon tea and tennis when the little barroom-type doors of the Judson College office swung quickly open. Dr. Merlin Kingsley entered. A woman in the early forties, she was dressed in white, spotless, severely practical. She sat down as one who could stop but a moment. There was a need and a definite plan for meeting that need. Both were quickly stated, and she rose to go, leaving me to think it over. Her Ford touring car pounded away bearing her on an ever-hurrying round of healing and helpfulness.

Doctor Kingsley was a member of an old Anglo-Indian family dating back to the time when East India Company subalterns married into the best Indian families. Her old car was not due to any lack of income. The many needs she could meet demanded all her resources, physical and financial. Her mother was a widow. The family was large. The younger brothers and sisters were above the average in ability; they must have their opportunity. She had set herself to give it to them. A brother was at Oxford preparing to be a barrister. He was a Tennis "Blue" and later became a member of the British Davis Cup Team. A sister was in University College, Rangoon. She was preparing for study abroad. She later returned as a teacher in her alma mater. Other members of the family would need her assistance. That was only one responsibility. In the ten years I had known her she had been continually adding to her responsibilities.

Doctor Kingsley had been trained and inspired by Dr. Marie Cote. This former missionary had blazed a path for women practitioners in Rangoon. After study abroad Doctor Kingsley returned to take up this practise when Doctor Cote laid it down. She had carried it on to even wider reaches of service. She was an alderman, the first woman to hold that office in Rangoon. Much time and strength went into the fight for public health and against white-slavers. In Immanuel Baptist Church she was the leading member, giving of her strength and resources without stint and winning a remarkable place with the young people. Sunday almost always found her at the organ leading the choir. Her preeminent service was, however, to the women and children of Rangoon. She was the city's leading obstetrician, entering a field occupied largely by ignorant, unsanitary midwives. The poor could always count upon her help. Utterly forgetful of self, thinking only of service to others, at her death in 1927 she was readily recognized as the first citizen of Rangoon.

A Rangoon funeral furnishes an unusually accurate index of the place occupied by the deceased. The coolie in his simple winding-sheet is borne on a humble bed. A wealthy Hindu funeral has its brass band, an elaborate hearse, and thousands of coppers thrown to the crowds. At the interment of the Burmese man of wealth his friends stand at the cemetery gates distributing presents. Doctor Kingsley's cortege had a significance all its own. His Excellency the Governor placed a wreath on her casket. The Lord Mayor of Rangoon, scores of those in high places, and hundreds from humble homes followed the body to the grave. Never had been seen such an outpouring of all classes, creeds, and nationalities expressing the sorrow of a city. Doctor Kingsley walked in the footsteps of her Master.

Another Christian physician is Dr. Ma Saw Sa. She is now Rangoon's leading woman physician. Many in America saw her at the Jubilee services. To really appreciate any Oriental woman, however, one must place her in her own setting. Dr. Ma Saw Sa is exquisite of dress and has a dignity and charm of manner all her own. To see her walk across the lawns at a government house-party is to see one manifestly distinguished among the citizens of a great city. She is a third generation Christian, the daughter of a high government official. She attended Judson College in its junior college days. After graduation from Calcutta University Medical School she went abroad as a state scholar. She returned from the University of Dublin with two degrees, F. R. C. S. I. and D. P. H., which mean in "American" a well-qualified M. D. Being the first among Burmese girls to gain this distinction, she in a peculiar sense has become their ideal. Many girls are today planning to become doctors due to her making the medical profession attractive. Dr. Ma Saw Sa's "The Clinic" on Tank Road, Rangoon, is full of promise for all Burma.

The Moulmein Hospital

The Burman Mission's efforts to meet the health needs of women and children have found their chief expression in the Ellen Mitchell Memorial Hospital in Moulmein. Arthur Darrow came to Moulmein the year after Doctor

Mitchell's death. She had for twenty-two years carried on a little hospital in a house on the hillside. That house became the Darrow home. There were continual reminders of the ever-present needs which Doctor Mitchell had met. Mr. Darrow's work was among the Talaings, rulers of Burma in the early days. Four years after his arrival there was a large ingathering into the Talaing church. As a thank-offering two decades later, this group raised Rs. 10,000. They purchased a fine site and at the Judson Centennial in 1913 presented it to the Foreign Mission Societies. It was to be used for medical work for women of all races. There near Mt. Hope now stands a fine hospital and a nurses' home.

When the hospital was opened in 1918 many people were suspicious of foreign doctors and their remedies. It was difficult to get them to remain at the hospital for treatment. Today that hospital is crowded with patients. The nurses' home is filled with a fine group of girls in training. These nurses go to all parts of Burma to meet one of that country's greatest needs. Two of them may be taken as examples of the rest. Miriam is in the Mongnai field helping Doctor Gibbens in his hospital. Daisy Gaung E has gone back to Nyaunglebin. She cares for the ills of the boys and girls in the large mission boarding-school. She advises mothers and ministers to many community needs. There are five Americans, three doctors and two nurses, at Moulmein. Their combined impact is of tremendous importance. It is by no means limited to the four walls of the hospital. They go to a number of villages to give health talks and to hold religious services. Dr. Grace Seagrave, daughter of Albert E. Seagrave, for many years an able adviser to the Rangoon Karens, recently helped welcome the twin sons of a teacher in a village school. Though the couple were Buddhists, that help from a Christian physician opened the doors of their home. Sixty children now gather there each week for Sunday school.

The Leper Asylum

It is from this hospital that the doctors come to help the lepers. Doctor Mitchell went to the cemeteries where Burmese custom banishes them. For many years now, however, there has been a growing asylum. It is carried on through the cooperative efforts of the American Mission to Lepers and the local people of Moulmein. One of the missionary men is always superintendent. The treatment which sometimes heals this most loathsome of diseases is given by one of our hospital physicians. No more self-sacrificing ministry can be found than this.

The Rest Haven at Taunggyi

There is yet another ministry, the plans for which began in Moulmein. The first Judson College boy I met was Jimmy Sandys. He was a freshman, an Anglo-Indian, one of "Saya" Kelly's boys from Mandalay. Later I found him in my logic class. An impediment of speech hindered his recitations. His paper work was by all odds the best of the class. Gradually there came the vision of his taking my place at furlough and my going to meet other urgent needs. That stammering stood in the way. But many hours of labor brought improvement till the time came when he successfully taught freshman logic. Then the white plague laid hold of him. Almost before we knew it he was gone.

Many such heart-breaking experiences at Morton Lane School, Moulmein, brought a conviction. Miss Lizbeth Hughes and Miss Agnes Whitehead, two seniors in missionary service, dreamed of a rest haven. In 1927 it became a reality. Taunggyi is high above sea-level with a climate of the finest. Many girls with tubercular tendencies have gone up from the plains to find health in this home. Since it was opened, only four years ago, more than fifty girls have been cared for, and all but two are going on with their work now. Such a haven has a value incalculable.

Women's Bible Schools

Burma's side of the Bay of Bengal has never known India's curses: suttee, infanticide, child marriage, and enforced widowhood. Burma knows nothing of obscene, idolatrous rites, nor of the worship of

> The organs of birth and circlet of bones,
> And the light loves carved on the temple stones.

Women as freely as men listen to the itinerant evangelist. The urgent call for zenana workers has never come from Burma. Yet there are missionary women, like Rangoon's "Mama-gyee," Anne Frederickson, who have made a marked contribution in full-time evangelism. Today a tiny chapel stands in the shadow of Mandalay Hill. Through services and Sunday school, Bible-women and nurses, there is brought home to Buddhist women an idea "of Christ's all-forsaking love." In this both Burmese and American women have a part.

The two Bible schools, the Karen in Rangoon and the Burmese in Insein, are training a capable group of women for just such an outreach. With ninety in one school and twenty-five in the other, a three-years' course sends out well-trained evangelists. It is no easy task these women face. Ma Mya May from her tiny house on the Burmese Mission Compound in Toungoo tells of her efforts in the school. A boy asked to be baptized against his parents' wishes. He was taken out of school. Life was made miserable for him. He wanted the Bible-women to get him work. "All we can do is pray that he may stay true and that we may be able to help him in this terrible time of need." Another, Ma Chaw from the village of "Forty Houses," declares in her quaint English: "I always praying, I must be clean, I must be pure, looks just like dove." So she presses on, spending a large portion of her very meager salary in order that the work may prosper.

A new source of support for the Bible schools has been found in the two Women's Mission Societies, the All-Burma and the Karen. Both of these organizations are comparatively young. Both contribute toward the expenses of the schools. What is more important, both pay salaries of graduates who go to all parts of Burma. Their presidents, Ma Mya and Ma Mi Lon, are most capable. Their fine faces give unmistakable evidence of consecrated lives.

The Missionary's Wife

In any sketch of the work of American women in Burma the missionary's wife must be given a major place. Ann Hasseltine Judson worthily heads the list. Possessing courage and devotion of the highest order, she stands as a peer of her distinguished husband. Her little group of women meeting "on Wednesday at seven" in those early Rangoon days brought to Christ Mah Men La "the tenth Burman convert, and the first woman. She was indeed among women what Moung Shwa-gnong was among men, of most extensive acquaintance through the place, of much strength of mind, decision of character, and consequent influence over others." Indeed to that little meeting may be traced six of the first seventeen hard-won members of the Rangoon Church. Christian women are often a minority among the Burmese. Among the Karens they are usually in the majority, so making the more "normal" church. Over a thousand of them are teachers in Baptist mission schools. Over two hundred are full-time evangelists. The coming to Christ of many of these women is directly traceable to the missionary home. From Tavoy to Namkham, from Sandoway to Kengtung, in hospital, school, and home the women of Burma are contributing as full a share to the Christian cause as their sisters anywhere.

"Ann of Ava" by no means stands alone among missionary wives in sacrifice and accomplishment. A glance at the service record of the first Thomases gives another picture of deepest devotion.

Missionary reports are usually made by the men. Neither missionary magazines nor letter-files show many communications from the missionary wife. One does occasionally find such a letter as that written by Charlotte Bacheller Thomas picturing their first jungle journey out from Tavoy in January, 1852. It was by elephant "with a motion too much like a ship to be pleasant." There was camping by pure streams of water, in dense forests, at the base of lofty mountains. There were devotions in English and Karen, and experiences which brought deep happiness to their little tent, for " Christ is even here." So goes the charmingly written account of just one of many such trips through the years in Tavoy and Henzada.

There is, however, another journey typical of the actual in the life of more than one missionary, and of the possible for all missionaries in the first seven or eight decades of the Burma Mission. This trip must be pieced together from bits found in her husband's last letters.

Benjamin Calley Thomas went to Bassein from Henzada to heal a rift between the Karens and the mission. That last year found him in January, 1868, regretfully recording his inability to complete the eighteenth year of his first term of service. Mrs. Thomas " has not recovered from an attack of cholera." He himself is " reduced to almost a skeleton." These two, with Willis, their son of twelve, leave Bassein on January 30 to return to America by the " Overland Route "—steamer to Penang, thence by way of Point de Galle, Ceylon, to Egypt, and by rail through the construction camps across the Isthmus of Suez, it being two years before the opening of the Canal. Nine weeks from Bassein finds them on the steamer Tangore near Marseilles with this comment on his health: " I have been far from well all the way." Ten days later in Paris, " my sickness has rather increased than diminished. My family are better or at least no worse." Three weeks later he is " a very little better " and can cross to England. From London on May 9 he declines an invitation to speak at the " May Meetings " in America because " I really believe it would kill me." Finally on June 8, after eighteen weeks of intense anxiety, Mrs. Thomas arrives with him in New York City, only to have him succumb two days later.

BAPTISTS IN BURMA

Yet the combined ancestry of Miles Standish and John Alden sent that devoted lady back to Burma to continue for more than twenty years her self-forgetful service. Her son, Willis, joined her in 1880 to carry on in his father's stead for forty-five years.

The way in which many such a missionary wife and mother has made the home a veritable beacon set on high, makes no more than just the "full missionary appointment" accorded her by the Board. One such "only a missionary's wife" is referred to by Sir Walter Roper Lawrence in his *The India We Served* (1929) :

The women in Burma all hope to be men in the next transmigration, and I heard of a missionary lady near Prome who was much liked by the Burmans, but the reason they took her medicine so readily was not that they believed in her skill as a doctor, but because they were certain that by virtue of the laws of Karma she would become a man in the next world.

The one mentioned by Sir Walter is Harriet Calista Stevens, daughter of Francis Mason. She, for forty-five years, ably aided her husband, Edward Oliver Stevens, in presenting Christ to Burma. That dear lady notes this bit of unsought praise with "I was amused to see this reference to me. The part I liked best was the fact that I was much liked by the Burmese. Love begets love. They knew that I loved them."

As one in the twentieth century reads "Ye are the *light* of the world" there comes to mind neither candle, nor kerosene lamp, rather an incandescent bulb, an almost invisible something within a fragile covering which, when touched with power, sends its rays far and wide. So the "Light of the World" clearly manifests himself when he touches within its fragile covering that invisible something, the soul of a woman, for then his rays are thrown afar by the very light of her countenance. Nothing demonstrates more clearly the power of the gospel than where that crystallized hardness, instilled by Buddhism, is broken and there shines forth the full beauty of Christ from the countenance of the Burmese woman.

VIII

MEN AND METHODS

U San Baw: District Secretary

At a distance on the path in the Pegu Yomas he appears to be an official. He is seated on a swaying elephant. He wears a khaki colored sun-helmet of the pig-sticker type. The background of tree ferns and giant feathery bamboos gives a striking setting. But he lacks the official's retinue. Then, too, he rides his Indian " ship of state " as one to the manner born. There is an easy yielding to the mighty beast's motions. He is not tossed on the choppy sea which the elephant usually makes for the man from the West. As he comes closer one sees he wears a blue jacket and bright-colored *longyee*. The elephant kneels, and a stalwart figure steps easily down. The smiling face and kindly brown eyes are those of that outstanding Karen, U San Baw, executive secretary of the Tharrawaddy Karen Association. He is returning from a missionary " voyage " to the churches high in the eastern hills.

U San Baw is one of " Mama " Higby's boys. After twenty-two years as the head master of the Tharrawaddy school he ran for the Legislature. The other candidate was a Buddhist lawyer, whose slogan was: " Fellow Buddhists, vote for one of your own race and religion. Don't vote for a Christian Karen." But the Christian Karen won. The Tharrawaddy school, though under Karen management, welcomes Burmese students. In the Legislature U San Baw cared for the interests of both races. In

recognition of his services Government awarded him the
" Kaisar-i-Hind " medal.

Since 1923 he has been in charge of the evangelistic
work among the Tharrawaddy Karens, a task which
formerly fell to a missionary. There are forty-three
churches to be visited and encouraged. Two new churches
were organized and a new meeting-house built in 1929.
While in 1930 there were one hundred and twenty-one
baptisms, forty-nine of these from Karen Buddhist families. That year also saw a wide variety of efforts for
furthering church growth. Eight vacation workers
preached in eight villages. A ten-days' Summer Assembly was conducted entirely by the Karens. The Tharrawaddy Home Mission Society employs fourteen workers.
There are in addition six Bible-women, four Christian
Endeavor secretaries, and two traveling evangelists. All
but one are supported by the Karens. Tharrawaddy is
just one of many vigorous associations in Burma.

The United Effort of All Races

The Burma Baptist Missionary Convention—the cooperative effort of all races—also renders outstanding missionary service. The " missionary " in its name is simply
to indicate its effort to bring the knowledge of Christ to
every unreached corner. American missionaries form only
one-sixth of its committee of management. Among its
officers are found a Karen, a Burman, and an Indian. Its
mission workers are scattered from Tavoy on the south to
the far northeastern border. There U Ba Thaw cares for
churches among the Myitgyina Lisus. Over in Siam under
the leadership of U Ennie Dewar they are pressing the
evangelization of the Karens. Near Thayetmyo among

the Chins the Convention supports a teacher-preacher, U Po Sein. He works in Hnitkyatkwe—one of those easily remembered names. On a similar task they send U Ba Tun far north, two days beyond Namkham, among the Shans. Nor are the Chinese forgotten; in Mandalay U Pak Hang teaches during the school year and spends his holidays preaching in many places in Upper Burma. The record of Burma Christians in catching the missionary vision of their American associates gives them high rank among the "younger churches." Yet their vision of the place the church should occupy, their knowledge of what it has done for them, makes them plead for more American missionaries.

The Need for New Missionaries

The "Opportunities for Christian Service" list of the Student Volunteers shows that the Foreign Mission Boards of North America are planning to send overseas a total of 778 missionaries during 1931. That number by no means covers the urgent requests. Other really "desperate needs" must be placed on a "Secondary List." Northern Baptists through their Boards present a striking list of needs they have set themselves to fill. There is not one of their fields but what has sent urgent requests. These include evangelistic advisers to local pastors, evangelistic leaders of advance into scarcely touched areas, teachers to train future leaders, and physicians to do the above in addition to their ministry of healing.

Burma has many races. There have been remarkable ingatherings among the hill-folk. The multitudes in the valleys have been much less moved. All three factors enter into the pleas from Burma for 1931. Away up in the Chin Hills is a real stirring of interest among that frontier race. It may mean that many Chins now animists will become Buddhists. It is more likely that they will become Christians. That is if the gospel is given them. During the rainy season a little Bible school of twelve is being conducted in Haka. There is literary work to be done. There are many weary miles to travel. It is little wonder there comes a repeated plea for "Another family for the Chin Hills." Mandalay, the center of Burmese Buddism, needs an evangelist. Assistance must be sent to care for the mass movement among the Lahus and Was across the Burma border. The President of the Burmese Theological Seminary cannot continue indefinitely to divide himself between two fulltime positions. He should have help among the immigrant Indians. Then, too, Judson College urgently needs replacements for the losses from its staff. A like plea comes from the Pwo Karens. There are 625,000 of them. They have such outstanding leaders as U Toe Khut of Maubin and U Shwe Ba of Bassein, both members of the Legislature. They urge that a second family be sent. They want this missionary to inspire and to counsel them, and also to help them win their non-Christian neighbors who otherwise will become Buddhists. Such are just some of the needs. The Baptist churches of Burma are every year assuming larger responsibilities, yet the Baptist churches of America must continue their help, if the rich promise of the future is to be fulfilled.

The Type of Candidate Required

In meeting these needs depleted treasuries are a difficulty, but an even greater difficulty is the finding of enough men and women really ready to go. A new vision is needed. Candidates there are, but not enough who are able to meet the requirements—spiritual, mental, and physical. The last sometimes seems the most difficult. More than one couple has come ideally qualified spiritually and mentally. Then comes the medical examiner's report. They have been found unfit for the severe test of a tropical climate. The other requirements of foreign service are far from being easily met. Try, for example, to find among your acquaintances any who could satisfy the set of specifications as given in the replies of twenty-seven Mission Board executives. A check list was sent out by the Editor of *Far Horizons*. It "assumes that a Christian experience and conviction is the magnet core about which all these qualities will be coiled." The summing up of the replies given in the October, 1930, issue finds five qualities with the highest rating. They are: cooperative ability, unbiased appreciation of other races, genuineness, capacity for growth, and sense of mission. This order of rating, as well as the qualities specified, has thought-provoking power for any one interested in the church's task overseas.

If today's group of American Baptist missionaries do not measure up—there are unbiased critics who declare they do—it is not because of lack of care in their choice. Today's candidate reference blanks are sent to people who know the candidate well. They give confidential information by checking characteristics through the list covering some sixty-five groups bearing on all aspects of character and qualifications. No one knows better than the modern missionary administrator that "the missionary enterprise finds its largest power and its largest peril in its personnel." This is even more true today than it was in the earlier years of the endeavor. Missionaries today are " the most severely selected group of workers now in the Christian movement, and they show it." Become a world traveler, seek out the missionary in his adopted land, and you will agree with this comment. If he does not always seem so when found on furlough, remember the degree to which his native country has become for him a foreign land. Then, too, don't forget how quickly we Americans condemn any one who is " different."

Elias William Kelly: The Right Type

The second decade of the twentieth century saw still in Burma missionaries whose service dated well back into the nineteenth century. The writer has always counted it one of his great privileges to have known that truly remarkable group of men and women. If one must be picked as the type a missionary should be, let Elias William Kelly be taken as that representative. His name must be placed high on any world list of Christian workers. Josiah Nelson Cushing transformed " Rangoon Karen College " into a cosmopolitan institution. Doctor Kelly conducted the negotiations with Government and consummated the preliminary plans which made it possible for that institution to become " Judson College " and to have the fine group of buildings which it has today.

Missionary Methods

Cushing and Kelly should also be bracketed together as leading protagonists of schools as a missionary method. Probably no two men did more to make for schools the large place they now hold in the Burma Mission. Though these schools involved large grants-in-aid from Govern-

[113]

ment, they still defended such a relation between Church and State. They maintained that Christian schools are an essential and effective method of accomplishing the missionary purpose. The only way open for conducting such schools was in cooperation with Government. Were they right in giving education such high rating as a missionary method? On this point Burma should give a clear answer.

The Burma Educational Code

Government regulations have practically compelled the opening of mission schools. Any such schools have been required to come under the provincial educational department. Government does maintain some schools directly from public funds. In addition, most municipalities have established schools. Yet many more must be maintained particularly in the villages if the Christian children are to have any education. State control is exercised through inspection and grants-in-aid. What America would consider a first responsibility of the State is in Burma left largely to the initiative of the people in any community. Many schools, Buddhist, Hindu, Moslem, and Christian, have been established " under private management." There have been, until recently, no restrictions on religious teaching. These schools have made possible the intimate union of secular and religious education within the walls of one building.

The Vital Place of the School

Mission schools have made a large contribution to Christian progress. They not merely train children from Christian homes. They actually win many boys and girls to Christ. As to the cooperation of Church and State in their conduct, Baptists have insisted that no church school in America receive public funds. This position is soundly based, but it is based on experience. When experience in Burma shows that the system is working injustice, it must be changed. At present it is the only means possible of securing justice. Otherwise the vast majority of Christians would have no schools.

Of Burma's 888 Baptist Mission schools 611 are for the Karens. These Karen schools are located in almost every case in villages wholly or largely Christian. Often the same set of men are the village elders, the church deacons, and the school trustees. Not more than one-half the cost of the school is returned to them out of their own taxes. The balance is met by school fees and subscriptions. Entire freedom to teach of Christ is unquestioned. From these schools has come the Karen leadership. The results have been remarkable.

A Kachin Christian Village

Among the Kachins the forces for uplift have also centered about the Christian chapel-school. Each is a tremendous purifying influence. That the Kachin in his natural state needs some outer cleansing, there is no shadow of doubt. Rumor has it that a hospital nurse had to bathe a Kachin three times before she reached the epidermis. That cleansing to be permanent must start from within. The end of the road on which William Henry Roberts, veteran missionary, took me gave undisputable evidence of the vital place of the village school. We set out one April day to visit Christian villages back over the high mountain passes in the Lungshan Valley on China's border. Our destination was four days' journey by pony from Bhamo. Along that mountain path were many demon-ridden villages with their filthy streets and filthier houses. Everywhere the two horsemen with their four pack-mules were met by groups of curious children. Each seemed dirtier than the last. They were sturdy, likable lads, many of them. More than one had a furrow down his chest where some water somehow by accident had trickled. He had just that much more water than was his due. Anything approaching adequate ablutions should only come at birth, at marriage, and at death. There were Christian villages which were vastly different, particularly the one at the end of the trail. It was N'Bapa, the outstanding Christian village of that district. Started some years before, it had grown as Christian families from other villages had moved into it. Set on a hill in the bend of a stream, it was surrounded by orchid-festooned forests. Its streets and houses were of the quintessence of neatness. The picture it made that morning is unforgetable. Running down to meet the missionary party came a bit of a boy. He was dressed in typical baggy trousers and jacket, both of cotton, both dark blue and both clean. Another outward evidence of inner change was a face rubbed bright with Sunlight soap. As he came he sang:

> *Yesu ngai hpe tsaw ai ra.*
> Jesus loves me. This I know.

So hundreds of lives are being remade. N'Bapa is but one of some sixty such villages. Children formerly trained to be cutthroats are now becoming true Christians. The return to the cause of Christ from these village schools is beyond reckoning. The future of the Baptist church in the Kachin Hills is bright.

MEN AND METHODS

Government and Schools in the Chin Hills

Statistics sometimes deceive. For the hills and valleys around Haka the 1924 mission report gives nine schools with three hundred pupils. In 1930 there are reported only three schools and seventy-five pupils. That mission work there has gone backward seems evident. The fact is, however, that a Baptist missionary, Herbert Cope, is Honorary (which means unpaid) Inspector of Government Schools. The newly appointed subinspector was the head master of the Haka mission school, a Karen Baptist. Some thirty schools with fifteen hundred pupils form the circuit. The teachers are all Christian. Their spare time is spent winning pupils and their parents to Christ. The Honorary Inspector spent 280 days on tour last year. Almost every night he preached in one or the other of the several dialects. While on this long trek text-books have been written. A hymn-book and the completion of the translation of the New Testament into Chin might also be mentioned, just to show that the schools are by no means his main interest. These schools are entirely supported by Government. By this cooperation schools are kept open which otherwise must have been closed. They are better housed and equipped. They are better staffed than Government alone could possibly have staffed them. For they have appealed to down-country Karens as a real missionary task. Their Christian impact is immeasurable.

The Leavening Influence

Much might be said of other schools among other races of Burma. The teachers in all the schools of the mission are almost without exception Christians. This offers the

I   [117]

Christian parent what he so much desires. He is reluctant to send his children to schools staffed largely by Hindus, Buddhists, and Mohammedans. In some of the mission schools Christian students are in the minority. This makes it difficult to maintain a strong Christian atmosphere. The rise of national feeling has not decreased this difficulty. If the nationalist slogan should change from " Burma for the Burmans " to " Burma for the Buddhists " the question of the continuance of certain of these schools may become acute.

Another very important aspect must not be overlooked. Through the schools there has been a great leavening of Buddhists with Christian ideals. One may find evidence of this in many places. Arthur Mayhew, able member of the Indian Educational Service, insists that this leavening in India has eliminated all reason for fear of " any antagonism to Christian missions as the outcome " of the change in government and the placing of more power in the hands of the people. Burma's experience so far would support this opinion. Opposition to Christian schools led by Buddhist priests has at times arisen. The results might have been disastrous but for kindly disposed Buddhist leaders. Mission schools have been a large factor in creating this friendly attitude.

Some Odd Missionary Methods

There have been various other missionary methods. Raymond Lull some six centuries ago crossed the Mediterranean to convert the Moslems of North Africa. He carried with him three concentric circles of pasteboard. These were each divided into nine sections lettered B, C, D, etc. By the manipulation of these letters the truth of

Christianity was to be proved to the doubting disciples of Mahomed. He tried his new method in Tunis. At the age of eighty he became a martyr. When his symbolic logic failed, he launched a " tumultuous " attack which speedily brought his end.

In a somewhat similar manner but fortunately without such disastrous results Jonathan Wade purchased in Calcutta an orrery. This apparatus is designed to illustrate the movements of the earth about the sun. Wade believed " that if they were convinced that their ideas of astronomy were false, their whole system would stand a confessed system of falsehood."

Nathan Brown, eminent missionary linguist, not only in Burma but also in Assam and Japan, fell into like error. He declares, " Let a Burman only believe that there is such a country as America, at a distance and of a size corresponding to our description of it, and his faith in Buddhism is annihilated at once."

The Chief Method Is the Living Voice

Fortunately only a few men either in those early years or today are tricked by too much learning. Not many have lost sight of the main missionary method. And they have done so only for the moment. Eugenio Kincaid, a century ago, ably expressed what has been recognized by all, Wade and Brown included, from the earliest days down to the present. Kincaid testifies : " The longer I continue among the Burmans the more I am convinced that the gospel conveyed by the living voice is the means appointed for the conversion of men. Reading of books enlightens, and induces a spirit of inquiry; but the full and overflowing heart reaches the conscience, and awakens the finer feelings of the soul. Hence the necessity of preaching the word, of being instant in season and out of season. It is not enough that we pray for them; it is not enough that we give them books; we must preach Jesus Christ, and not be discouraged amidst reproaches and insults."

Evangelistic Work Involves Hardships

E. W. Kelly, the champion of schools, gave many of his richest years to evangelistic work. There is hardly a letter from him to the Mission Rooms in Boston but this, his one purpose, no matter where he is stationed, is manifest. Both the college and the evangelistic work are good, " but surely the evangelistic return is the better," he declares. Always he is pressing for a " forward and aggressive movement" in evangelism and ever urging increasing appropriations for reaching more villages. He continues: " I can work every month in the year in the district if I only have funds. It means work, *toil,* it means exposure, great exposure in the rains; it means all my capacity for anxiety and care and patience, but I believe it means success under God. Make me as your servant and brother to add to the great number who have been led to Christ through your prayers and efforts."

One might write much of Kelly's connection with Rangoon, Moulmein, and Mandalay, with Cushing, Judson, and Kelly High Schools, the last now named for him, and especially with Judson College. There were sermons preached to English congregations that would easily have won high position in American pastorates. There were hands extraordinarily adept in unraveling snarls in church, school, or mission affairs. With his ability in council he might easily have mounted high in diplomatic circles.

MEN AND METHODS

Rather than following the usual biographical lines, however, let us get instead an intimate glimpse of the spirit of the missionary. Pen pictures have been drawn of missionaries courageously facing the danger of violent death. Tropical disease can be equally dangerous. Between the lines of this note to a Board Secretary read real courage. Many a man would have fled before the danger this missionary unflinchingly faced.

RANGOON, DECEMBER 12, 1896.

DEAR DUNCAN:

I am compelled to write you that my health has become seriously impaired. Early in August I took cold, from getting wet while traveling. As a result I had to call a physician, a civil surgeon, during the last of September. He took me through two attacks. In the last of October I had a still more severe attack. Doctor Kirkpatrick cared for me for ten days, night and day, and pulled me through. He did most excellent and brotherly service. I was able to go to the district one trip in November. On December 3, I started again, but after six days had to return with a fresh attack of dysentery that threatened to be very bad. . . Doctor Kirkpatrick says the trouble is catarrhal inflammation of the liver and dysentery—both climatic and a bad complication. From the beginning the troubles have shown a *persistence* that has never once yielded fully. I get better, but not well.

Yours faithfully,

E. W. KELLY.

Such were the hardships cheerfully faced, for were not the returns " more than one hundred and thirty baptized in town and district " so far that year?

Two Different Gospel Tracts

Even in evangelistic effort there has been a diversity of methods. This can not be better shown than in the little tracts, very important tools in breaking ground for cultivation on the mission field. One well-known tract of the earlier years is the "Investigator." This through questions and answers makes cutting comparison of Christianity and Buddhism. Answer One insists that it is not proper to ask how God began, a question any keen-witted Buddhist monk would immediately propound. Answer Eight denies omniscience to Gautama because he, forsooth, declares that no man could know the beginnings of things. "Of God it is not proper to ask the question where and how he came to be." Of Gautama, "if he is not able to see anything of the beginnings of things, how is it going to be said that he knows all things wholly?" So it proceeds to state that the Pitakas, the Buddhist scriptures, are hearsay set up by the priests to promote offerings—what modern terminology would call religious graft. The "Investigator" closes with a reference to the prophecy that "before long every false religion will be destroyed, and in every place in the world the 'mill-lay-nee,' which establishes the Kingdom of Heaven, will come." Few Buddhists reached this, to them, cryptic reference to the millennium, for of this tract one missionary writes: "Some hatred was manifested this morning. One was torn to pieces and thrown into the river as soon as my back was turned." The "Investigator" is long out of print. With it should be compared "The Golden Balance." This tract is Adoniram Judson's own. It is still on sale and is asked for by Buddhists who have heard it praised by their coreligionists. It contains comparisons of Buddha and Christ, but they are exceedingly kindly comparisons, waiving for the moment the truth or falsity of the glories ascribed to Gautama. It just takes him as they believe him to be,

THE
GOLDEN BALANCE

ရွှေချိန်ခွင်စာ။

RANGOON:
AMERICAN BAPTIST MISSION PRESS,
H. W. SMITH, SUPT.
1928.

Stereotyped 40th Edition-10,000-327,000Ω.

JUDSON'S OWN TRACT
Still in Demand

and places him beside the One whom the missionary calls Master. Let the life of Christ speak for itself is its theme. So Judson more than a century ago employed a method which modern students of missions declare is the proper " Christian approach to non-Christian religions."

A Missionary Veteran's Vision

This latter, the finer and better way, was the one in which Doctor Kelly instructed me, a new member of the faculty at Judson. I had been out only a year when he first came as president in 1911. The simple, direct presentation of Christ and the gospel with only occasional, always kindly, comparisons with Buddhism was his method. By this method he had made notable advances in evangelism.

In the last eighteen months of his life Doctor Kelly, due to declining health, handed over the administration of Judson College to that new faculty member of ten years before. The frequent visits of his successor, continually seeking his sound advice, found the " Sayagyi's " fervor never faltering. In fact, it burned even brighter as his physical powers waned. On the veranda of the Burman mission bungalow in Rangoon, a house secured through his oft-repeated pleas over a long number of years, he sat through those final months, a lonely figure. Much of the time was spent reading his Burmese New Testament. He was too feeble to return to America to join his wife who was held there by ill health. Though his end seemed clearly written in his enfeebled frame, he never for a moment lost his fine faith and courage. In conversation his face would light up as he told of a bit of a village on the banks of the Sittang River where he hoped he and

Mrs. Kelly could live, of the house, just a little village home like the rest about it, where, when he was well enough, he would go to spend his remaining days just telling Burmese Buddhists about Christ. Such was Elias William Kelly, for many years the Mission's leading advocate of schools.

IX

A PROPHECY FULFILLED

The Judson Centennial

Five "little girls" were the peak point of the Judson Centennial celebration in Rangoon. Four of them had fathers with records of more than forty years each in Burma. These same four daughters had themselves each an active service average of more than fifty years. All five could remember the years following 1840. That December day in 1913 Sarah Stevens Smith, Mary Brayton Rose, Julia Haswell Vinton, Susan Haswell, and Sarah Stilson became again little folk seeing the face and hearing the voice of Adoniram Judson. The last of the five, Sarah Stilson, speaking with a youthful enthusiasm not one whit dimmed by her seventy-four years, declared:

Though the pioneer has passed, his work is going on. New churches, new industries, new schools are springing up till Burma promises to be honeycombed with the influence of Christian missions. Village after village shall sing:

> *Chay zoo daw go thi gyin sow.*
> Hymns of praise to Grace Divine.

A survey of the almost completed first fifth of the second century more than justifies this optimism. In addition some new forces have assumed a real share in the accomplishment of the task, the fulfilling of the prophecy.

Since the Centennial

The seventeen years since the centennial have seen 502 new churches; 368 churches become self-supporting;

251 new schools. Of these schools almost all are new village Christian centers. Contributions from the churches in 1913 were $92,000. In 1930 these contributions had mounted to $258,000. School fees in 1913 were $44,000 while 1930 saw that item reach $252,000.

Of new buildings many of the larger ones have been already mentioned. Scores of smaller structures involving great self-sacrifice on the part of the churches might be enumerated. Among the Burmese in the Thonze field Letpedan, Tooywa, and other outstations have built acceptable chapels entirely from their own funds. The Shwegyin Karen field has recently undertaken a heavy program. With a membership that only totals about two thousand five hundred, they are launching a building program amounting to Rs. 74,000/.

Taking Burma as a whole the new church buildings reach a high total. Bamboo structures have been torn down to be replaced by very sturdy and substantial, if not particularly handsome, teak buildings. In other places old, dingy brown meeting-houses of teak have been replaced by modern brick chapel-schools. Insistence on self-support has made development along certain lines slower. But after all the sturdy oak cannot be grown in a hothouse.

Among the Burmese Churches

Pause a moment, and see the progress in and about Pegu. Merrick Parish by unceasing evangelistic effort has since the centennial increased the number of churches from one to seven. Their membership has grown from eighty-one to three hundred and fifty. Numbers do not mount rapidly among the Buddhists. It requires an ever-persistent pressing of the message to individuals; that same method which Judson employed in garnering his first nineteen. Pegu also has a well-organized Home Mission Committee. Its secretary is U Tha Aung, the pastor of the Pegu Church. His church ably, and entirely independent of missionary leadership, entertained the Burmese Association recently. In Burma entertainment still means just that. They have not adopted the " pay as you enter " system prevalent in America.

Just a glance at two other Burmese fields. Swing up over the heavily forested Pegu Yomas. Drop down on their westward side into the heart of the Irrawaddy Delta. Here is an area also crowded with high-metaled, proud people. Since the turn of the mission century the schools in Thonze field have increased from six to sixteen. That means ten more centers of Christian influence in important villages. The same may be said of Henzada's fifteen schools. Each is a chapel on Sunday, a schoolhouse the rest of the week. Through this seven-day training plan the Christians are being brought to a position of leadership in their communities.

Hospitals for Burma's Valleys

Let us turn then to the new forces which are assuming a share in the accomplishment of the missionary objective. One of these has been mentioned, the Ellen Mitchell Memorial Hospital at Moulmein. Doctor Mitchell's own little hospital has also been referred to. With those two exceptions there has been no sustained medical work in Burma proper during the history of the mission. Here as in education the mission has been influenced by Government policies. Government hospitals have endeavored to care for this need, because of this mission medical work has not been so urgently necessary.

Admittedly an Indian Medical Service man is stationed at each district headquarters. These men are either British or Nationals trained abroad in the best British schools. They conduct civil hospitals and some additional dispensary work. Very recently the Burma Government has also cooperated with the Rockefeller Foundation in a demonstration of modern health organization. This experimental unit is located in a village twenty miles north of Rangoon. The further extension of this work would mean untold benefit to countless villages.

Some estimate of the adequacy of the Government medical service may be gained by a look at the Chin Hills. In that hill tract of twelve thousand square miles with a population of 120,000 there are three Government hospitals. These are staffed by a Civil Surgeon and eleven subassistant surgeons. Three of the latter travel about in the villages some twenty days in the month. In other words, one medical worker to ten thousand people scattered over one hundred square miles. An adequate mission program should include a doctor for these hills.

The Government of Burma must be commended for its efforts to provide medical relief for the people. Still there remain many places beside the Chin Hills where the services rendered can hardly be considered adequate. Even granting that they are all that any government might be expected to attempt, still one must regret that there are not more mission hospitals. Burma should have more of that powerful appeal of the Master given only as through his physicians " the blind receive their sight and the lame walk."

Physicians for the Frontiers

To place physicians everywhere is hardly possible. To give some concrete expression to Christ's compassion for human suffering is almost indispensable. This has been done on Burma's frontiers. American Baptists have sent in all fifteen physicians outside the province proper to the frontiers. They have been stationed high up in the Himalayan foot-hills which form the rim of Burma. Truman Johnson served long and ably at Loikaw in the Red Karen country on the east. After his death Mrs. Jennie Bixby Johnson bravely carried on for a decade. Then that medical work ceased. Erick East and John Woodin, both fine physicians, were between them for eleven years at the hospital at Haka in the Chin Hills. Then it closed its doors. The heavy demand on mission resources has not made it seem wise to try to continue it.

In the Shan States there are now missionary doctors at Taunggyi, Mongnai, Kengtung, and Namkham. Twelve mission physicians have through the years ministered to the Shans. Five of these have been at Namkham. One finds there today the new Harper Memorial Hospital with Gordon Seagrave, a great-grandson of Justus Hatch Vinton, in charge. This hospital is a memorial to his predecessor, Robert Harper, the man with the burly body and the big heart. The old hospital had " a Christian influence which cannot be measured with a hundred-mile yardstick." How much more effective the new hospital must be! The old was " a dark gloomy building on stilts. The floors were covered with stains of blood and pus and medicines which had soaked into them during the twenty or thirty years. They were made of soft spongy jungle wood, and no amount of scrubbing would make the floor clean." The new building is of native stone. It is light, airy—and above all, it can be kept clean. This hospital is one of the new factors of the new century. It, like Moulmein, trains a corps of nurses. They have gone here and there through the hills and valleys carrying an ever-widening ministry.

The future of the church in no small part rests on the question whether there may be found other Christian physicians, both men and women, to give themselves for the upbuilding of Burma. Dr. L. T. Ah Pon has served the mission long and well in the Shan States. Hope for others lies largely in those whom Judson College is sending from its premedic course to become Bachelors of Medicine of the University of Rangoon.

Zewaka: The Celebrated Burmese Physician

The ignorance of the average man of the East in matters of Western medicine is, as might be expected, appalling. True, the eclectic *zay saya* has discovered a number of valuable remedies. Chaulmoogra oil, long known in India and China as a remedy for skin diseases, was sold in the bazaars of Burma many years before Western science employed it for leprosy. Government has undertaken the codifying of these discoveries. The celebrated physician Zewaka, who " once cured a colic which afflicted the Lord Buddha Gautama, by simply giving him three flowers to smell," is the father of Burmese medicine. No examinations are required of his followers.

The charlatan has a wide open door for his frauds. Examine one sample from his medicine case, a common remedy for bad sores.

(1) The "hand" of a *taukete,* the big trout-spotted lizard that haunts the thatch of houses. (2) Sulphur. (3) The bulb of a white lily. (4) A chili roasted. (5) Cock's dung. Mix in equal parts, and stir while heating it, and finally add some earth oil.

Hanson finds in Kachin pharmacy, "Among other drugs, the blood of wild buffalo, the gall of a python, the fat and gall of the slow-loris, crushed tiger's bones, musk, and the gall of the bear are especially valued."

Waste-Basket Surgery

A striking instance of "Practising Medicine and Surgery—and How!" in the Kachin-Shan country is found in that fascinating book of Gordon Seagrave's *Waste-Basket Surgery:*

A man came for an abdominal operation, localized peritonitis. We had none of the drainage materials used in America. All I could find was a rubber tube, hard and brittle. And I stuck that in for a drain. Three days later it was nowhere to be found. I was terrified. I was certain we should have to cut him open again. He said it had been bothering him a little, and he had pulled it out and thrown it away. We were convinced that he was lying, but we decided to look around first before doing anything so drastic as to cut him up again. We walked from ward to ward, looking for it under the beds and in the corners without success, so you can imagine how perfectly delighted we were when we got out on the front porch and found a baby using that tube for a pacifier! He had almost pacified himself permanently.

Brought up on "the more bitter the better," any physician, civil or missionary, with sugar-coated pills finds his path difficult; yet experience proves that the Christian physician can open doors closed to others.

A PROPHECY FULFILLED

Unmet Medical Needs

Not only in the Chin Hills in the far northeastern corner of the country is Government unable to meet the need, but few of the tens of thousands of villages have anything approaching adequate medical treatment. Even Rangoon, the best equipped of any city of the Province has only a civil hospital of five hundred and fifteen beds and a Sri Rama Krishna hospital of one hundred beds for a city of almost four hundred thousand people. The followers of the Hindu mystic are to be commended on their open-minded acceptance and active exemplification of Christ's message of service to all. Yet, too, they are a challenge to the Christian Church to help provide the " at least five hundred additional beds very urgently needed " for Rangoon. In this Dr. Ma Saw Sa is ably doing her part. Through her efforts the religion of Jesus Christ is living today as it did in the ministrations of Doctor Mitchell in Moulmein, and Doctor Kingsley in Rangoon.

Burma's Effort to Aid the Rural Billions

A second venture of the second century was the Pyinmana Agricultural School. It is Burma's bit of evidence of a new approach to an old problem. The World Missionary Conference in Edinburgh in 1910 did not in any way consider the special needs of rural areas. The Jerusalem Conference of 1928 devotes a volume of its findings to " Missions and Rural Problems." It is not that there has been an Oriental " Back to the Farm " movement. It is but a new realization of the old economic problem, a problem that in Burma, as in all Asia, is largely written in rural terms. Of Burma's thirteen million, nine million are engaged in agriculture. There are only some seventy towns as compared with thirty-five thousand villages. In these the farmers live. The isolated homestead is entirely unknown. India has an average of 225 people to every square mile. Burma has only about a quarter of that number. Yet even in Burma the problem of making ends meet is acute. Two pairs of bullocks and their quota of land—twenty-eight acres—should in that " garden spot " give a family a fair support, but they do not know how to reap the full benefit of the rich soil. Months of abundance are succeeded by months with a shortage of proper food. There results a lack of stamina to fight disease. For the most part the cultivator knows only a single crop—rice. The many months between the annual harvests tend to debt with interest at 50 per cent. or more per annum. This soon devours the twenty-eight acres. Large numbers of land-owners, Christian and non-Christian, are becoming tenants of the *Chetties,* " natives of India "—Shylocks— who foreclose at the first opportunity.

Granted that the development of the church is sorely hampered by poverty, what business is that of a foreign mission society? " None," would have been the answer of most of us two decades ago. The economic side of life lay outside our conception of the missionary task. Yet, somehow, a vicious circle must be broken. Consider the question in a most limited sense. The path to permanence is churches. Self-support is essential, if they are to be truly indigenous. Poverty prevents self-support and presses for mission doles. Such doles develop flabby muscles unprepared for that heavy upgrade climb to devolution of mission responsibility. Yet you may say— " Look at the marvelous accomplishment of the Karens."

Comparatively speaking, they have given themselves better
equipment than is to be found almost anywhere East or
West. Yet the Karens, increasingly, wish that phrase,
" comparatively speaking," removed. Why should not
Ein-chain-lay-zee have what any " 40-house " village con-
siders essential in America—in church, in school, and in
adequate medical care? And they will get these things for
themselves, provided they can be pointed to paths of
higher physical and economic as well as higher spiritual
levels. In fact, it is difficult to see how they can attain
the highest spiritual levels without a radical reconstruction
of living conditions.

A Burmese Village Transformed

Pyinmana's first task is making better farmers of those
who have already found Christ. In no sense does it set
itself to furnish material inducements for entrance into
the church. Yet that agricultural school inevitably piles
up weighty evidence in favor of the Christian religion. Its
portly pigs point the way of escape from poverty which
" stunts the soul." Buddhism concerns itself largely with
nauk pawa, the next existence. Christianity serves " the
whole man in every aspect of his life and relationships."
Some say " that the Kingdom of God cometh by preaching,
and others by education, and others by making two blades
of grass grow where only one grew before." Seventy-five
boys at Pyinmana through a four years' course are getting
training in all these, so that they may return to their
villages, there to give the combined impact of all three
bringers of the Kingdom. Pin Thaung is a sample village.
It was " the worst of the district, full of opium-smugglers
and opium-eaters, rice-whiskey distillers and drinkers,

gamblers and cattle-thieves." Yet it is rapidly becoming completely changed. It now has a Christian headman, a good school, and a church of one hundred members. All this because the people were prepared to heed the message of men whose advice had transformed their rice-fields.

A large part of Pyinmana's expenses are met by Government grants-in-aid. Thomas Jesse Jones' expert judgment is that " in these days of national self-determination and racial consciousness cooperation with governments and nationals is almost the *sine qua non* of permanent and genuine service, rural or otherwise." Pyinmana has that cooperation.

Student Gospel Teams

So much for pigs and pills. Now for play and its striking part in Kingdom advance. Any one from the tropics knows that a set or so of tennis is a tonic much needed to stir sluggish blood. Soccer football leagues such as those in Rangoon's "allied schools"—the Normal, English High, and Cushing High Schools—are stirring the sluggish blood of a nation. These leagues include Midgets, Junior-juniors, Juniors, and Seniors. They bring to any one closely connected with them a firm conviction of the value of games. Besides physical vigor, they produce those invaluable incommensurables—a sense of fair play and a spirit of cooperation. To these the second century has seen other high values added. The student gospel-teams since 1923 have found a place for play as a key to prejudice-bound Buddhist hearts. They have brought to Burma her first recognition that the sharp smack of a boxer's glove may clear the way for Christ's entrance into a hitherto indifferent heart.

A STUDENT GOSPEL-TEAM STARTS REVIVAL IN INDIA

A PROPHECY FULFILLED

Thousands of Buddhist pupils enrolled in mission schools have attended daily Bible classes during their formative years. Their minds have been filled with Christian truth, but their hearts have too often still been held fast bound by Buddhism. These groups have heard the plea of the missionary, of visiting teachers in school campaigns, and of such ardent general evangelists as William Hosmer Hascall and Willis Frye Thomas. For the most part, though they have been deeply moved, it has not been quite to the point of acceptance. From such faithful sowing the gospel-teams are reaping rich harvests.

New Evangelistic Methods

In this new movement play performs a double function. First of all it has brought about a marked change of attitude on the part of the Christian student. He had done evangelistic work before chiefly from a sense of duty and with no striking success. Now, impelled by " a heavenly joy " found in a method better adapted to his temperament he leads many into a knowledge of Christ. Then, too, " the vivacious, volatile, pleasure-loving, happy-go-lucky Burmans " have almost inevitably thought of Christianity as a barrier to that festivity which is such a large part of their Buddhism. Gospel-team campaigns have shown Christianity to be " The Way " along which they can take that joy and laughter they so much love. The campaign begins with a football or basket-ball game when the visitors from the metropolis meet the local team. The as yet unpicked partner in a Burma tennis tournament is often entered as "A. N. Other." The student athletes on the gospel-team always strive to play as if Another sat on the side-lines, for victory is gained only if friends are won for Him. There follow on successive nights a concert with perhaps a bit of boxing, a pageant, and a drama. This play appeal forms a happy approach to the deeper things—Bible classes, searching talks, and stirring personal testimonies. Each student evangelist tells of Christ's place in his personal experience. Before the close comes the drawing in of the nets. The method is that of personal appeal in a place apart, that of the well of Samaria, not that of the saw-dust trail. All these efforts are fused into one mighty impact by the warmth of "expert friendship." For the gospel-team credo is "Friends with God. Friends with each other. Friends with all others."

More than two hundred students—the very finest—from Judson College, the Burmese, Karen, and English Theological Seminaries, and the Karen and Burmese Women's Bible Schools during the first seven years of this movement have gone out as members of gospel-teams. Chief among the values is the indelible impression left on the lives of each of these students. In the campaign comes a deep emotional experience such as seems taboo among many of the "older churches" in America, yet the youth of the "younger churches" are proving that it may have an important place in this present day.

The worth-whileness of it all can perhaps best be seen in the light of the testimony of Johnson Kangyi, outstanding Karen, athlete, scholar, and glee club leader, now Assistant Professor of English in Judson College. His testing-time came while studying in America:

There was a very rude awakening when I was thrown against some Christian divinity students at the University in America, who said that my faith was irrational, childish, and blind. But when doubts and temptations assailed me, the vital religious experiences I had gone through with the student gospel-teams stood me in good stead. One of these students, not an American but an Indian Christian, insisted upon that ultra-rationalistic view of the Bible and life, so that there was no room for the living Christ; but I *know,* because others and I have proved it in our gospel-team work, that God is my Maker and Father, my Saviour and Friend.

X

READJUSTING RELATIONS

Burma's Immigration Problem

Monday, May 26, 1930, must be marked in black on Burma's calendar. It saw the beginning of racial riots. For five years India had been shaken by many sanguinary encounters between Hindus and Moslems, the chief apparent cause being the "cow-music" question. Burma's national bird, the peacock, had preened itself in "its pride proper," as it were, entirely superior to such communal clashes. Then there broke a terrible storm of arson and murder. Coringhee coolies from the Coconada coast of the Madras Presidency were the stevedores loading ships in Rangoon's crowded harbor. Their pay for that strenuous labor was fifty-four cents a day; they struck for sixty-two. The Burman had always scorned such menial labor. But the continued piling up of an unsalable surplus of rice made him eager for any employment. Here was a means of support which he thought was permanent. Skill and strength to handle large bags of rice do not come in a day. Coolie maistries wearied of the Burman novices and conceded the Coringhee demands. That Monday the just-discharged Burmese met the taunts and missiles of the triumphant Madrassi. The detested "native of India" had cut them off from sorely needed income. Consequences common to such industrial situations everywhere ensued. That is common except for their intense ferocity. Burmans from town and district ran amuck. Any Coringhee—man, woman, or child—risked death by venturing on the streets. Jinrikishas were wrested from their Indian pullers, smashed, and their axles employed as weapons. Soon, no *kala,* white or black, was safe from the brown man's wrath. Valiant efforts of British officials and Burmese elders together with the calming presence of His Majesty's Highlanders finally secured a cessation of hostilities; but not until more than one hundred had been killed and many times that number seriously injured.

Burma's welcome to unlimited numbers of cheap laborers from across the Bay has been definitely withdrawn. For years coolies by the hundred thousand (408,000 in 1926) have entered her ports for seasonal labor. More than ninety per cent. of them have returned to India each year. The rest, together with Indians of other classes, now number almost a million permanent settlers, about one-tenth of the population of Burma proper. Apprehension has been growing that Burma would soon lose her own individuality. Then came the pinch of financial depression, precipitating the inevitable clash. Such communal strife will continue to be a menace so long as Burma must submit to unrestricted immigration. The racial riots brought sharply to the fore the need for a readjustment of relations with India.

Separation from India Is Recommended

As he walks across an English racing paddock leading his winning horse, Rustom Pasha, one would not for a moment suspect him to be Aga Sultan Mohomed Shah, G. C. I. E., G. C. S. I., K. C. I. E., LL. D., spiritual head of Ismail Mohammedans. The wealthy and powerful

"Aga Khan" is also an authority on things Indian. His query, "Is Burma to be India's Ireland?" is worthy of most serious consideration; at least it was until June 24, 1930, the date of the publication of the second volume of the Simon Report. Sir John Simon's Royal Commission was appointed to inquire "into the working of the system of government in British India." Its Report recommended the immediate separation of Burma from India. Provided that recommendation met with the approval, first of the Round Table Conference and then of Parliament, prospects were bright for Burma. But would it secure such approval?

Envious eyes are turned toward Burma both from the west across the Bay of Bengal and from the east over the high Himalayan foot-hills. Edward Thompson in his exceedingly able *Reconstructing India* writes:

Practically all schools of Indian thought are opposed to the separation of Burma. The reason is economic. Burma is lightly populated; its struggle for existence, a thing of recent years, is due to the rapid silting of emigrants from India. India is over-populated, is debarred from East Africa and Australia, is eagerly looking for a land into which to dump her surplus folk. Independent India, presuming that its population continued to grow far beyond its power to support, would not resist the temptation to do with Burma what Japan has done with Korea.

The Round Table Conference in London proved this prophecy only partly correct. Thompson had not reckoned with the Indian Princes. That momentous conference met in the winter of 1930-31. It included Hindu and Buddhist, Moslem and Christian, caste and outcaste, ruling prince and common citizen. They came together with members of the British Parliament to consider India's future constitution. It had been thought that British India alone would wish dominion status. It seemed certain that the powerful Native States of Indian India would wish to retain their present direct relation with the Viceroy. It became clear early in the conference, however, that the maharajahs wished to join a federated India. These princes also favored the separation of Burma. The weight of their influence brought an early recommendation that Burma's plea be granted.

Burma Is Not India

The Burman easily finds a wealth of reasons why he should not be swallowed up in any future federated India. Burma is geographically distinct. Wide seas and high mountains covered with almost impenetrable jungle separate it from India, its neighbor on the north and west. None of the former conquerors of India ruled Burma. It was the British raj " purely as a matter of administrative convenience" who first did this. It is an unnatural alliance and should not be continued.

Burma faces east, not west. It looks toward China, not India. Its major races came from far Cathay. It is not like India, either Aryan or Dravidian. It has the marks of a Mongolian ancestry and civilization. Burma has no caste, no use of the veil for women, no early marriage nor an enforced widowhood. There are none of the major evils of Hindu society. In Burma the Buddhist monastery has made literacy almost ten times as great as in any other province of India. With the entire freedom from caste have come a gracious hospitality and a kindly tolerance. Add to these a natural light-heartedness and generosity, and you have " an individuality very delightful and valuable to the outside world." This individuality is threatened with extinction in any union with India.

Indian Actions Irritate Burma

India's favored treatment of its own cotton and steel industries together with its tax on the rice trade has been exceedingly irritating to Burma. Heavy import duties on cotton and steel have helped Indian mills but have added to Burma's burdens. For Burma has no steel nor cotton mills. Burma has rich oil-fields and valuable forests but its real wealth lies in the rice from its paddy plains. Anything that affects the price of rice is felt in every corner of the province. Some years ago an export duty was placed on rice by the Indian Legislative Assembly. This goes to India's central treasury for all India expenses. Of these expenses Burma's part is small. The Assembly in order to meet an acute slump in the rice trade in 1930 grudgingly reduced this duty about one-fiftieth of a cent a pound. A half million additional tons left Burma's paddy bins within two weeks. Popular belief is that that trifling reduction did it. Being the only Indian province to export any rice, Burma demands complete control of any duties that may hinder the sale of what is to it, in more senses than one, the staff of life.

Military Strength Made a Major Issue

In Burma sentiment is practically unanimous for separation. British parliamentary approval may be safely predicted. So far as opposition other than Indian is concerned, it centers itself on those envious eyes on the East in Siam and China. Siam once felt the heel of Burmese conquerors. The alarmists fear it would seek revenge

on an ill-defended Burma. China like India is over-populated. It might well covet Burma, that most blest by
nature of any land of the East. Any Rangoon fruit
market will give a glimpse of nature's bounty in Burma.
Bananas of a dozen varieties, as different in taste and
texture as the apples of the West; pomelos, a glorified
grape-fruit; sweet limes, an orange the size of a musk-
melon; apples filled with a fine fruit custard; mangoes
and mangosteens with nothing in the West worthy of
comparison; and last, but first of them all, the dorian,
with its delightful creamy fruit cheese and its odor " audi-
ble " at a hundred yards. Without question any nation,
East or West, would find Burma a profitable possession.
Its peace it is asserted could not be maintained without
the assistance of the Indian army. That army is almost
entirely British officered, so the problem of defense, it is
argued, is for British hands. The northwest frontier up
toward Turkestan has been the chief cause for serious
concern in India. It can hardly be called a Burma menace
except on the assumption of a complete collapse across
the Bay. Any arguments against Burma's ability to de-
fend herself may be applied with even greater force to
other provinces. The Punjab's bewhiskered battalions
are sixty-two per cent. of the army recruited in India.
Bengal furnishes not a single soldier. Burma the " prin-
cess of the provinces " contributes three thousand men.
True, Burma looks largely to the martial races of India for
its civil and military police. Burmans have fitted none too
well into the Indian military establishment, largely, it is
alleged, because it is too meagerly paid. Burmese recruit-
ment was cut in 1929, in part at least, because Indian
sepoys are cheaper. Burma's recruits are mostly Kachins,

Chins, Lisus, Marus, and other men of the Hills. These
"Burma Rifles" have an excellent record as garrison
troops, and, too, they have won distinction, for Subadar
Major Lasang Gam, ranking officer of the Kachins, a
Christian, has been called to London to act as a King's
Orderly. "Theophilus" of the *Rangoon Times* argues
with considerable cogency that the Burmese should be
trained as the "second line" to be called in emergencies
when real action is required. They could confidently be
expected to take their full part where any actual fighting
is imminent. They could and would ward off any covetous
hordes from China or Siam.

The Legislative Council Has a Good Record

So much for needed adjustment of external relations;
what then of adjustments from within? It has been asserted on good authority that Burma's legislative body has
been "the most level-headed and utilitarian of the provincial Councils set up under the dyarchic régime." To
be sure, there are keen critics who assert that any advance
in self-government is impossible. Sir Reginald Craddock,
former head of the Burma Government, in his *Dilemma in
India* declares: "The spoiled children of the East, so
radiant in gaiety, so feckless in purpose, taking no thought
for the future, must be born again before Burma can even
enter the Dominion of Home Rule. The explanation lies
in the moral fiber, and Acts of Parliament are powerless
to supply it. It must be a plant of local growth." On the
other hand, equally able men urge that as "The history
of nearly every country which has thrown off the shackles
of foreign control shows some kind of rejuvenation," so
it will be in Burma.

As to the matter of moral fiber, every session of the Legislature has seen some Burman rise to propose a Prohibition measure only to have his motion defeated by the official bloc, the Government-appointed members of that body. To be sure, time alone can tell whether this plea for prohibition is a matter of morals or just a means of harassing government.

In this connection it is well worthy of note that Sir Joseph Maung Gyi was officiating Governor in the fall of 1930. He is the second native son to hold such an office in any province of India. His appointment as the first Burman Governor is a clear indication of the confidence which the King-Emperor places in the Burmese people. The most serious difficulty is the shortage of leaders. The increase in the number of Nationals allowed to enter Government service was at one time looked upon as an advance. It is now proving a hindrance to self-government. For many years the cream of the colleges has been drawn off into Government employment, most of the positions of a subordinate nature. These positions pay salaries much larger than any available for their less fortunate college classmates. A large group of Burma's best have thus become " British Brahmins " barred by their official connections from political activity. Important cogs in the machine " made in Great Britain " for giving good government and giving it, their powers have been devoted to strengthening the position of the paternalistic British raj. If some means could be found for making their assistance available, Burma could much more quickly build a self-governing dominion.

The importance of these readjustments of relations from a missionary standpoint can hardly be overstated.

Some firmly believe that they portend grave difficulties. It is the confident belief of others that these changes will make for freedom and opportunity of the Christian community. Experience so far shows an increase in the prestige and influence of the Christian church.

Burma's Strategic Place in Asia

A separated Burma bears real promise of becoming the hub of a very considerable Oriental universe. A missionary at home on furlough from Rangoon painted a very telling picture. Under his facile tongue Burma became the land where all the human currents of the Orient meet, meet to divide again and make their influence felt to Asia's farthest corners. Of Burma Rangoon stands as the great port city, as the undisputed metropolis, the point at which this world-influencing function makes itself most felt. The aforesaid missionary's position placed him at the center of Rangoon. From which it was inferred, though not spoken, that his influence ran throughout the length and breadth of Asia. Whatever may be said of the final conclusion of this thesis, the premises cannot be seriously questioned. Many have come to Burma from the most widely scattered parts of Asia, they have found there sufficient of this world's goods to be able to return home in comparative wealth. So the fame of Burma has penetrated from the Punjab to South China, from Darjeeling to Singapore. The position she will come to occupy in the political life of Asia is a matter on which opinions may differ. Her unique economic position, due to her mineral resources, her forest reserves, and her paddy plains, is a matter of fact. And as for political predictions, Burma may in a few years easily loom largest in Oriental eyes of all countries east of Europe and west of Japan. Given separation, Burma " with its tolerance, its literacy, and its unity," unencumbered by the social conditions which hinder progress in India, seems certain to become a leader. It promises to blaze the way for the millions of subject peoples in Southern Asia. Success in self-government in Burma will furnish an unanswerable argument against any one race dominating another.

The Transfer of Administration in Baptist Work

To what degree have twelve decades of mission work prepared the church to play its part in this new Burma, soon to be? That eminent administrator, William Isaac Chamberlin, Secretary of the Board of Foreign Missions of the Reformed Church, has said that there are four stages in the history of foreign missions: First, the Mission; second, the Mission and the Church; third, the Church and the Mission; and finally, the Church. Burma is in large part in the " Church and Mission " stage. Administrative responsibility is being delegated to Joint Committees. They distribute funds for schools and evangelistic work. Missionaries to the Karens have long been, to a large degree, acting in an advisory rather than an administrative capacity. Some, for years, have had no more power than a State Convention Secretary. Karen elders have assumed responsibility not only for local affairs, but through their Associations for their home and foreign missions. In most fields they have advanced far toward self-direction and self-support. Joint committees are no novelty to them. The call of Thra San Ba, B. A., B. D., from the Seminary by the Bassein Sgaw Karens points clearly in the direction of complete church control in that great field. Burmese Christians, on the other hand, are fewer in number. They are gathered only in small groups. There are no Burmese villages entirely Christian. So they have not found it possible to assume as much responsibility. The Burmese Committee, therefore, finds many more schools and churches, which formerly looked to the Mission, still looking to it for support, than does the Karen Committee.

Each Joint Committee has a membership of nine Nationals and three missionaries. The high caliber of the Nationals may be seen by a glance at the personnel. On the Burman Committee are U Ba Hlaing, B. A., LL. B. (London), Moulmein Barrister, and U Hla Bu, M. A., Assistant Professor of Philosophy at Judson. On the Karen Committee are such men as Thra Maung Po, Henzada pastor, and Joseph Po M' Law, general evangelist for the Moulmein Karens. No National on either committee receives support from American funds. As for the missionaries, they are cooperating to place their present responsibility on the shoulders of Nationals, so that they themselves may press on to the large, as yet untouched, areas.

A Difficulty in Devolution

Devolution, the handing over of responsibility to nationals, is not easy of accomplishment for the missionary. Points where the answering of Burma's call most often causes missionary casualties are health and separation from children. This last has been greatly relieved by the excellent "American School" at Taunggyi. As to health, conditions have vastly improved through the years. Yet danger of disease is still much increased when one leaves

America for the tropics. Burma has not as yet become a bit of peaceful countryside. The year 1929 saw in the "bag" of its sportsmen 1,200 leopards and a like number of bears, 500 tigers were killed, and 400 elephants captured. There still remains more than a bit of jungle and much of the menace to health which jungle implies. Yet, after all, the chief drain on missionary strength comes in striving to combine efficiency and devolution. The Burman's favorite phrase is "at leisure"—the American's "busy." Ways of saying things often indicate ideals, and the ideals of the two peoples have differed just that much. Yet who can blame the tropical-born for craving leisure? How many Americans have cut short their careers trying to transplant "pep"? Perhaps, after all, the longer years and the slower pace will accomplish more. Still, for the missionary recruited because he was "a leader and organizer with energy, initiative, and self-reliance," few strains are more severe than to see that prized commodity, efficiency, endangered as he takes a second place. Is it a second place? David Chandler Gilmore, with long experience in Burma, feels "Devolution is going to mean that the missionary is to be promoted from the comparatively humble post of administrator, to the higher post of apostle, prophet, teacher. That is to say, he will be promoted, if he has it in him, through Christ, to *fill* these higher posts." Doctor Gilmore is among those already so promoted.

A Strong Church with Capable Leadership

But let us look at the church to which responsibility is being transferred. Adoniram Judson's goal was "to introduce the religion of Jesus Christ in the Empire of

[151]

Burma." On July 13, 1930, the one hundred and seventeenth anniversary of his arrival, there was held in Vinton Memorial Hall, the Annual Mass Meeting of the Rangoon Baptist City Mission Society. Twenty churches, totaling almost five thousand members, were represented. Six different tongues joined in "All Hail the Power of Jesus' Name." Surely this is evident that Judson's goal is gained.

Or, pass in review a few of Burma's fine group of Baptist leaders. In Rangoon, there are such men as Thra Pan, director of young people's work among two hundred churches in the Karen Association, and U Ba Han, pastor of the Burmese Church founded by Judson. He also teaches on Seminary Hill, Insein, with Saya Tha Din as an able colleague. Bassein brings memories of Thra Lugyi, fluent in three languages, fearless preacher to Buddhist Karens, and with him U Ba U, former Buddhist priest and now evangelist to the Burmans. Among the laymen are U Ba Tsoe, Burmese timber merchant, deeply devoted to the Pyinmana Church, and Thra Thin who bequeathed to the Bassein Association Rs. 30,000 for carrying the gospel to the Karens in " the regions beyond." Thra Kra Su is shouldering major responsibilities. " Old and rugged but a regular saint of God, he is carrying on in Loikaw where missionaries have found it hard to work."

Judson College points with pride to its graduates. Among its men are such mission school heads as U Po Win of the Moulmein Karen High School and U Po Min of the Myingyan Burman High School. There are, too, among its women Ma Hannah, fulltime secretary of the Daily Vacation School movement, and Ma Nu, a teacher in the Burmese Women's Bible School. There is also an impressive list in Government employ. U Than Tin and U Shwe Sein each hold that important post, somewhat misnamed, " Under-secretary to Government," Silas San Wah is a Judge in Mergui, and U Maung Cho is Provincial Inspector of National Schools. There are also U Ba Htin, Assistant Deputy Commissioner at Pegu, U Po Chit, headmaster of the Government High School at Insein, Daniel Aung Bwint of the Rangoon Police, and L. Htin Po, Civil Surgeon at Shwebo.

Maymyo Bible Assembly

No group better portrays the prospects for the future than those gathered at the Maymyo Bible Assembly. High in the hills east of Mandalay is Maymyo, Burma's summer capital. Here is the hot season residence of the Governor. Here, too, the Baptist Mission has an all-nations' church and a fine school for girls. Chief of the mission's buildings is the Milton Shirk Memorial Rest House. It gives rest and respite from the heat of the plains to many missionaries. Just across the road from the Rest House is the spacious assembly building. Ten days in late March and early April each year are given to this gathering. More than two decades of experience have proved its importance to the whole mission. The year 1930 saw twenty-three out of thirty-one mission stations represented. There were among the delegates sixty-four Burmans, sixty Karens, fifteen Anglo-Indians, five Chins, four Chinese, three Kachins, three Talaings, three Indian Christians, two Shans, two Hindus, one Armenian, two Taungthus and one Mohammedan. This racial roll-call indicates that every important group is being touched. The general subject was in 1929 " The Life without

Limit" and in 1930 "The Overcoming Life." There is a definite attempt to avoid that which has occupied the group, most of whom are students or teachers during the preceding nine months. The urgent need is not a wide and varied curriculum, rather spiritual renewal which will carry through the coming year. Bible classes in English, Burmese, and Karen, courses in C. E., and D. V. B. School methods and training in personal work occupy the mornings. The afternoons are given to recreation. In the evening is heard an inspirational address. On the closing Sunday afternoon in 1929 a consecration service was held out under the trees. Many lives were rededicated to Christ. Several for the first time made a public profession. All left the meeting with a deeper certainty of the place the Master must have in their lives. Foreign Secretary J. C. Robbins, deeply moved by what he saw and heard, declared, "When you can have such a meeting led in such a beautiful way by a Burmese pastor like U Ba Han, there is no need to fear for the future of the Kingdom of God in Burma."

Large Areas Are Still Unoccupied

A glimpse of these different groups almost leaves one persuaded that the task is done—persuaded till one turns to a few comparisons. The best record is among the Karens with, if Catholics are omitted, one in nine Christian. Among the hill-folk twelve thousand five hundred Christians are quite a company, yet the task which awaits is sixty times that number. Immigrant Indians are, many of them, Christians, yet only twenty-five out of every thousand have accepted Christ. As for the Burmese Buddhist the Christian bears a ratio of just one in one thousand. This ratio is substantially the same among the Shans. These figures point to many unoccupied areas. The districts of Ruby Mines, Katha, Upper Chindwin, Magwe, and Minbu have been but little touched. The Arakan division with nearly one million people finds the Bible Churchmen's Missionary Society taking up work in the north, an area neglected since the early days of the Baptist Mission.

Much is yet to be accomplished. Societies, other than the American Baptists, striving to help are the American Methodists in Lower Burma at Pegu and Rangoon together with Thongwa and Syriam close to the capital. The English Wesleyan Methodists with seven stations are scattered throughout Upper Burma from Kalaw in the Southern Shan States to Mawlaik far up the Chindwin River. The Bible Churchmen's Missionary Society, in addition to their new venture in Northern Arakan, have six points north and west of Bhamo where, since 1924, work is being attempted in the territory first penetrated by Eugenio Kincaid prospecting for a link between Burma and Assam Baptists. In none of these stations, save perhaps Pegu, may the work be said to overlap. The Society for the Propagation of the Gospel—the Church of England organization—has seven stations; and the Seventh Day Adventists from America have three. This last Society is now penetrating up the Salween River above Moulmein. There are also in Rangoon the Y. M. and Y. W. C. A., the British and Foreign Bible Society, and the Salvation Army. Although these other Christian organizations are doing their part, Baptists must assume major responsibility for untouched territory. Prior occupancy of Burma places responsibility on them.

BAPTISTS IN BURMA

Baptists have twice as many foreign workers and six times as many Nationals giving full time to mission work as all other religious bodies put together. The 1,320 Baptist churches occupy a position of first importance. Yet it is manifest that the door of opportunity has only been partially entered. Burma has unique political possibilities. If these possibilities are realized, the Christian church in Burma is bound to wield a wide influence. Edward Thompson, before the Round Table Conference in London in the winter of 1930-31, declared that if that Conference should prove successful, it would furnish the best propaganda in all history for the peaceful solution of disputes between nations. And more,

They will strike the hardest blow that racial and color prejudice have received since the time of Christ. For the first time, an Empire dominated mainly by people of one blood will have found a way to incorporate on equal terms a vast people of blood and thought and religious belief poles apart from its own. It will open up new hope for depressed and discouraged peoples everywhere, and there can be no limit set to the regions into which its influence will go. It will have repercussions on the policy of every nation that owns a yard of territory outside its own borders, or has any dissatisfied minority within them.

The progress made by the Round Table Conference far exceeded expectations.

An Opportunity Unexcelled Anywhere

Separated Burma bears promise of becoming a leader along this path of peace and of cooperation regardless of color. Burma is already far more democratic than any other province of India. Burma's racial and religious groups are much more kindly disposed to one another.

READJUSTING RELATIONS

The dominant religious group, the Buddhists, are believers in a faith by far the most susceptible of all in India to the permeation of Christian teaching. Buddhist ethical principles have acquired new meaning due to the constant contact with Christianity. The common reply to Christian teaching is *a tu du be*—they are the same. This attitude has opened doors for a leavening uplift. Would that it had carried farther! Be deeply grateful that we find Burma facing her future with her two most important groups, Christian and Buddhist, not " poles apart " but prepared to work together for the welfare of " Mother Burma." Through this cooperation Burma will not only play an exceedingly important part in the political drama of Southern Asia, but it will speak for Christ as well.

Dean Charles Reynolds Brown, on a visit to Japan, one of the far points to which the teachings of Gautama Buddha have penetrated, joined a band of pilgrims to the shrine at Kamakura built to memorialize that son of a king who gave his all to gain enlightenment. Standing before the heroic figure in bronze he exclaimed:

The dignity of the majestic figure, the look of peace and ineffable calm upon the face, the air of repose—meets the hurried, thoughtless tourist as if to hush him into reverence and meditation. But— the figure is seated; the arms are folded; the eyes are closed. It is the calm of death.

" The calm of death " cannot sit at a round table conference drawing up plans for democracy. Gautama Buddha accomplished much. His creed condemns caste. It aids in the emancipation of women. He has kept the path to self-government cleared of great barriers which still stand in India. But the foundation principles for the new structure must be furnished by Another: the One who stands erect, his arms outstretched, his eyes alight. The need is not the calm of death but the light of a living love. Burma, coveted of men for their selfish purposes, is coveted by the Master for quite other ends. Will he possess it? The answer rests on the continued cooperation of the Churches in America and the Churches in Burma.

BURMA'S LION
Guardian of the Pagodas

QUESTIONS FOR DISCUSSION

CHAPTER I.—ADONIRAM JUDSON

1. Sketch the life of Adoniram Judson prior to his departure from America, catching contrasts with today.
2. Discuss the difficulties of Ann and Adoniram Judson in going to the foreign field. Compare them with those today.
3. What effect did the Judsons becoming Baptists have in the awakening and developing of that denomination in America?
4. Why should the question of immersion require long consideration by the Judsons and Luther Rice?
5. How is tropical Burma different from Northern U. S. A.?
6. Read Kipling's "Road to Mandalay." Is its geography correct?
7. What reasons, do you suppose, caused "the teacher" to delay accepting Christ?
8. How is Rangoon in 1931 different from Rangoon in 1813?
9. Name the Mission institutions in Rangoon. Are they all included within Adoniram Judson's purpose?

CHAPTER II.—VOYAGES AND MOTIVES

1. Name four differences between travel to the field in 1834 and today.
2. Why is life in Burma's frontier stations difficult? How is it different from the homeland?

[159]

3. Are all three missionary motives necessary? Are they enough?

4. Is Burma more "needy" than America? If so, how? If not, why not?

5. Name nine different races and the mission stations for each.

6. In what ways do racial differences increase the difficulties of mission work?

CHAPTER III.—FOUR ESSENTIALS

1. What are the modern missionary's main difficulties in learning the language? How is his task different from Judson's?

2. Why is Burmese more difficult to learn than French?

3. What are some by-products of language study? What is the value of each by-product?

4. How would you proceed in reducing a language to writing? What are some words difficult to catch?

5. What book would you most like to share with the people of Burma? Why?

6. Why was the Mission Board wise in sending Hough as Judson's first associate?

7. What Christian literature is necessary for America? For Burma?

8. How can Christianity avoid being called a foreign religion?

9. Why is the missionary task impossible of achievement by foreigners alone?

QUESTIONS FOR DISCUSSION

CHAPTER IV.—CERTAIN BARRIERS

1. Why were the Burmans hostile to Boardman?
2. Why were the Karens friendly to the British? To the missionaries?
3. Was Boardman right in turning his attention to the Karens?
4. Do you find anything to commend, anything to criticize in the three Buddhist objects of worship?
5. In what ways should Christianity be especially attractive to Buddhists?
6. Compare Gautama's journey to the Anauma River with Jesus' triumphal entry into Jerusalem.
7. What do the "Four Roads to Perfection" lack?
8. In what ways is Buddha's self-sacrifice different from Christ's?
9. Must a one hundred per cent. Burman be a Buddhist?
10. In what ways were the Karens a barrier to Burmese Buddhists becoming Christians?
11. What are some other reasons why Buddhists are difficult to win to Christ?

CHAPTER V.—COCOANUT CREEK KARENS

1. How did travel through tropical jungle for Abbott, how does it even today, differ from a hike through our forests?
2. The many missionary deaths in Arakan would not be considered justifiable today. Were they or are we right?
3. Should a church ask its "missionary pastor" to make greater sacrifice than its own minister?

4. Was the price paid for the gospel by the Karens too high? Do conditions among the Karens today give any answer to this question?

5. Why did the missionaries to the Karens move from Sandoway to Bassein?

6. Why did not the coming of the British doom the religion of the Burman?

7. What were the points of strength and of weakness in the early Karen leaders?

8. Of the three characteristics of vigorous church life— self-propagation, self-government, and self-support—which should come first in emphasis? Which second?

9. If the average wage of a day-laborer in Burma is Rs. 1/ per day, what would be the equivalent in dollars of Rs. 20,300?

10. Name the Karen Mission stations. How widely are they scattered?

CHAPTER VI.—BEYOND MANDALAY

1. Name the mission stations for Kachins, for Chins, for Shans, for Lahus and Was.

2. What sections of Burma does each race occupy?

3. How is the savage more religious than the civilized man?

4. Which is easier for you to understand, Animism or Buddhism? Why is this true?

5. Why do Animists accept Christ more quickly than Buddhists?

6. Is it fair to compare Kachin demons with Salem witches?

QUESTIONS FOR DISCUSSION

7. How is our superstitious "knocking on wood" different from a Kachin sacrificing a chicken?
8. How are the many dialects developed?
9. Would you think that recent immigration has been good or bad for Burma?
10. Should the Foreign Mission Society attempt to meet new needs, even if it goes in debt?

CHAPTER VII.—WOMEN'S WORK

1. Compare the purpose of Judson with the goal of the Woman's American Baptist Foreign Mission Society. Does the former include the latter?
2. What is meant by the "elevation of women"? How does Christian education contribute to this?
3. The girls of Burma are eager for education. What danger and what hope does this movement hold?
4. Compare the proverb, "Better a male dog than a woman," with Christ's teaching. How might such a proverb influence the attitude toward education for girls?
5. Remembering that much of Animism clings to Buddhism—Why should women be suspicious of foreign medicines?
6. What conditions make the training of women nurses an urgent need?
7. Why is leprosy the most dreaded of diseases?
8. Describe four Hindu customs never practised by Buddhists. How do these affect the position of women?
9. Describe the witnessing ministry of the Christian home.

CHAPTER VIII.—MEN AND METHODS

1. Name some natural difficulties which arise in combining several language groups in one convention.

2. In your judgment, what are the necessary qualifications of a missionary?

3. How would you proceed in order to procure candidates possessing these qualifications?

4. Just what is the task of mission schools? Should these schools continue if Government forbids required Bible classes and chapel services?

5. Is secular education a help or a hindrance to becoming a Christian?

6. Should mission schools in Burma receive financial aid from Government?

7. Should missionaries be divided into educational and evangelistic?

8. Have Christians in America any responsibility for giving a secular education to the children of Burma?

9. Is the leavening influence of foreign missions to be counted among its good results even though it does not lead to conversion?

10. Why is the living voice in preaching and personal work preeminent among methods?

11. What should be the attitude of the missionary toward the religions of Burma? Give reasons for Judson's " Golden Balance " being better than " The Investigator."

12. Would E. W. Kelly's abilities have been wasted in a village?

QUESTIONS FOR DISCUSSION

Chapter IX.—A Prophecy Fulfilled

1. Name the mission stations among the Burmese. (See Chapter II.) What areas appear to be uncared for?

2. Why is evangelistic work among the Burmans more difficult than among the Karens?

3. Is the ministry of healing one of the essential functions of our missionary endeavor? What part did it have in Christ's life work?

4. What is the purpose of medical missions? (1) To heal? (2) To win converts? (3) To "reveal the attitude of God toward men"?

5. In what ways would the practise of the medical missionary differ from that of your family physician?

6. Imagining yourself to be an Animist, why are tigers' bones good medicine?

7. "Foreign missions should train leaders for all departments of life: evangelistic, educational, medical, social, industrial, and political." Do you think all six of these departments of life should be included?

8. Discuss pro and con the advisability of sending agricultural experts as foreign missionaries.

9. Do you approve of the methods employed by the gospel-teams?

10. Should Christians from Burma be brought to America for further training? Do you think such visits will deepen their Christian life?

Chapter X.—Readjusting Relations

1. What are four major differences between Burma and India?

2. Should ability to raise armies be essential to nation-hood?

3. What should be the American missionary's attitude toward the political reforms now under way in Burma?

4. What factors make Rangoon the hub of a considerable universe?

5. Should missionaries insist on control of work as long as it receives support from America?

6. Should missionaries be sent out to work under the direction of nationals? Has U San Ba a right to ask of American missionaries what is implied in his "Call for Colleagues," in Chapter II?

7. What parts of Burma are still unoccupied by missionaries? What parts are inadequately taken care of? In the light of these facts discuss the statement: "Missionary work is less needed today than formerly."

8. What did Judson start out to do in Burma? Give some outstanding examples of evidence of accomplishment of this purpose.

9. How do Burma's political prospects increase the need for Christ?

BOOKS ON BURMA

General:

    Alexander McLeish. *Christian Progress in Burma* (1929). Paper, $1.00; cloth, $1.50. World Dominion Press.

    S. W. Cooks. *A Short History of Burma.* $1.60. Macmillan.

    Encyclopedia Britannica: Burma, Rangoon, Buddhism, Animism.

Burmans:

    Shway Yoe (Sir George Scott). *The Burman: His Life and Notions.* $5.00. Macmillan.

    K. J. Saunders. *Buddhism and Buddhists in Southern Asia.* $1.00. Macmillan.

    Adoniram Judson—Apostle to Burma. 75 cents. The Judson Press.

Chins:

    Mrs. L. H. Carson. *Pioneer Trails, Trials, and Triumphs.* Paper, 60 cents. J. H. Merriam, Pasadena, Calif.

Shans:

    Gordon Seagrave. *Waste-Basket Surgery.* $1.50. The American Baptist Publication Society.

Karens:

    Dr. San C. Po. *Burma and the Karens.* $2.50. Leland, 129 Park Row, N. Y. C.

    Rev. E. N. Harris. *A Star in the East.* $1.50. Lit. Dept. B. M. C., N. Y. C.

    Rev. H. I. Marshall. *The Karen People of Burma.* Paper, $3.00; cloth, $4.00. Ohio State University Press.

    Alonzo Bunker. *Sketches from the Karen Hills.* 75 cents. Revell.

BOOKS ON BURMA

Novels:

Honoré Willsie Morrow. *Splendor of God.* $2.50. Wm. Morrow & Co., N. Y. C.

F. Tennyson Jesse. *The Lacquer Lady.* $2.50. Macmillan.

Alonzo Bunker. *Soo Tha—a Tale of the Karens.* 75 cents. Revell.